THE DEAD EYE AND THE DEEP BLUE SEA

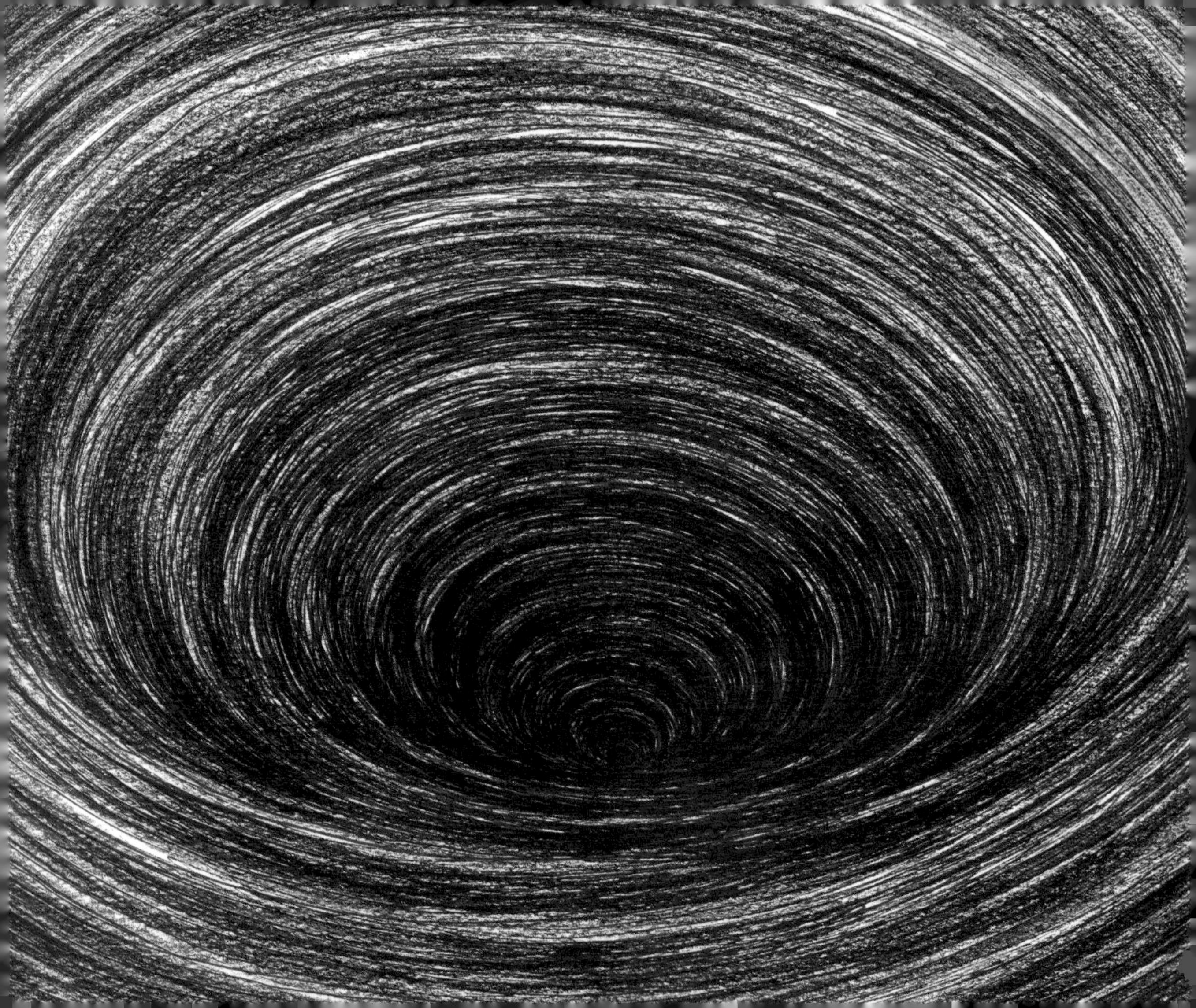

THE DEAD EYE AND THE DEEP BLUE SEA

A GRAPHIC MEMOIR OF MODERN SLAVERY

VANNAK ANAN PRUM

AS TOLD TO
BEN & JOCELYN PEDERICK
AND TRANSLATED BY
LIM SOPHORN

SEVEN STORIES PRESS
New York • Oakland • London

Foreword copyright © 2018 by Anne Elizabeth Moore
Introduction copyright © 2018 Minky Worden
Afterword copyright © 2018 Kevin Bales

A SEVEN STORIES PRESS FIRST EDITION

SEVEN STORIES PRESS
140 Watts Street
New York, NY 10013
www.sevenstories.com

Library of Congress Cataloging-in-Publication Data

Names: Vannak, Prum. | Pederick, Jocelyn. | Pederick, Ben.
Title: The dead eye and the deep blue sea : a graphic memoir of modern
slavery / Prum Vannak ; edited and translated by Jocelyn Pederick and Ben Pederick.
Other titles: Memoir of slavery at sea
Description: New York : Seven Stories Press, [2018]
Identifiers: LCCN 2014040483 | ISBN 9781609806026 (hardcover)
Subjects: LCSH: Vannak, Prum. | Fishers--Cambodia--Biography. |
Fisheries--Corrupt practices. | Tattoo artists--Cambodia--Biography. |
Plantation workers--Malaysia--Sibu (Sarawak)--Biography. |
Slaves--Biography. | Slave labor--Thailand. | Slave labor--Malaysia. |
Human trafficking--Thailand. | Human trafficking--Malaysia.
Classification: LCC HD8039.F66 C35 2018 | DDC 331.7/6392092 [B] --dc23
LC record available at https://lccn.loc.gov/2014040483

DESIGN
Stewart Cauley, Abigail Miller, and Carlotta Colarieti

Printed in China

1 3 5 7 9 8 6 4 2

CONTENTS

FOREWORD

IF YOU have spent any time at all in the quiet, eerie Tuol Sleng museum in Phnom Penh, Cambodia, you have felt something truly terrifying. In 1975 the peaceful, contemplative Southeast Asian high school was turned overnight into Khmer Rouge Security Prison 21 (S-21), a torture prison. Only seven people are known to have escaped with their lives by the time the Vietnamese invaded the city in 1979 to end the extremist regime. Today Tuol Sleng stands as a dusty place where more than 12,000 people died of violations so senseless you cannot, and do not want to, imagine them. The smells, the sounds, the stillness of the air, the makeshift artifacts of a regime that took power so quickly that functionaries had to invent new means of corporal punishment to maintain power over the impoverished nation: these are all present, comingling, uncomfortable. Torture methods were crude and merciless and meted out haphazardly. The happy solitude of neighbors near the museum living normal lives in a developing nation today testifies to and deepens your sense of horror at what happened in this place.

But nothing makes you feel it in your gut until you come across that first painting.

Vann Nath, the artist, the survivor, came to S-21 a prisoner, then bargained for a position in the regime. As an artist. He proposed to create portraits of key leaders of the Khmer Rouge and document daily life at the prison. He did precisely that. It is unclear what the Khmer Rouge thought such paintings would accomplish of benefit to the murderous government; they can only devastate. Simple human figures subjected to ghastly abuses by simple tools. The figures are not graceful—how can they be? They are often wretched. Stretched on a rack for waterboarding, hung on a pole, submerged upside down into a tank, held still while a guard snips off fingers. A baby smashed against a tree. Worse still may be those moments between abuses, daily life, when survival seems so un-likely: Vann Nath's self-taught hand casts a body in starvation and dehydration. The artist as wit-ness to the deterioration of human life before his eyes, placing it now before ours.

Vann Nath died in 2011, when he was one of only three remaining survivors of the seven to live though S-21. Can you imagine: at the end of your life only two other people had seen what you had seen. The responsibility to capture it. The guilt for sharing it. On top of questions about why it had happened at all, and how you managed to escape. The joy of creation, the catharsis of documentation; this was what saw you through. Thereafter, your life's work would serve as a reminder, or a warning.

Vannak Anan Prum's graphic memoir is a modern recasting of Vann Nath's paintings, a testament to their legacy; a document of contemporary and ongoing abuses that, while arguably less extreme, are certainly far more widespread. In images as simple and declarative as Nath's, Prum relays a similar tale of poverty-inspired torture and abuse; of lives pushed to, and beyond, all imagined extremes. These are stories that inspire rage and hate and fear in equal measures, but are told so thoughtfully in still, full-color drawings, that the images them-selves, despite the injustices they condemn, demand a solemn respect.

It would be imprudent to suggest that Prum was inspired by Nath; the story you are about to read relays Prum's nontraditional art education quite thoroughly, and it is an education com-mon to all the upcoming great artists in Cam-bodia, many of whom first learned to draw with sticks in the dirt. Some moved on to pencils and paper; others, like Prum, had little access to ma-terials, so used their own bodies to perfect the quality of their line. What truly connects Nath and Prum is that they were forced to explore aesthetics as a means of survival under intense physical duress and in a climate of unimaginable fear.

That Prum's work can be traced to Vann Nath's is notable, because there is also a rich history of comics in Cambodia, a form that, given the oppressive Khmer Rouge regime, tended instead toward romance. A long, healthy tradition, too: from Em Satya, who has published since the 1960s but grew to popularity with tales of young love in the 1980s, to Bonsovathary Uoeung, who still creates an occasional comic strip called "Ginger," based on her grandmother's recollections of silly moments from the country's constant political changeovers. It is rare for such an intensely poverty-stricken nation to devote itself to the printed form. Usually print is viewed as an extravagance when money is tight. I've spent several years in the nation reading and teaching comics, and several years in countries like the Republic of Georgia that operate under similar states of economic duress but have no such histories. Teaching comics in Cambodia is helping folks explore a medium they came to naturally. Elsewhere it is often a sheer novelty, if not a complete waste of time. Some of this can be explained by the large number of non-governmental organizations in the country in the aftermath of the Khmer Rouge regime; as they were gradually defunded, moved elsewhere, or were shut down by the democratic-in-name-only government, their photocopiers were sold off. "Freedom of the press is guaranteed only to those who own one," American journalist A. J. Liebling said. Cambodians used that freedom to copy even those works protected by copyright elsewhere, comics among them. While this made it difficult for artists to make a living from their work, it did foster a readership devoted to the form.

Prum relies on a readership already eager to explore aesthetics and narrative, viewers primed also by Vann Nath's intrepid depictions from the nation's darkest days. Prum is clearly comfortable combining text and image in a documentary—and often quite confessional—format, but he's bucking the tradition of Cambodian comics, or perhaps, bucking the tradition of a form that can only convey the travails of the beloved. Prum's drawings, a series of elaborate and beautiful testaments to a life lived *despite*, to survival under duress, detail instead the unwanted travels of men with no options who are rapidly losing hope. An entire economy is built on their unhealing wounds, on bodies that will never be found, on court cases that, in corrupt nations during these dark political times, will never take place. Prum's graphic memoir details a broken heart, yes, his: a heart broken by a world that doesn't care about labor trafficking or the maltreatment of brown men when there is profit to be made.

Vannak Anan Prum's story will make you feel these violations in your gut. What you do with that sensation is up to you.

ANNE ELIZABETH MOORE

INTRODUCTION

Surviving to tell the tale of "sea prison"
MY THREE sons have grown up reading—and loving—Marvel Comics, cartoons, and graphic novels. My boys, like their counterparts around the globe, fiercely debate the relative strengths of "Hulk" versus "Iron Man." Reading sketches in *Diary of a Wimpy Kid*, the pre-teen angst series, my boys emit peals of laughter. But not all the graphic novels depict hilarity or superpowers. Some bring the unimaginable to life. My oldest son read Art Spiegelman's *Maus: A Survivor's Tale* and learned about the scale of human catastrophe during the Holocaust. In this book, Vannak Prum has captured the horror of modern slavery at sea.

Art has power. Children's crayon drawings during the Darfur crisis in Sudan exposed the devastation that these children had witnessed: their villages attacked by helicopters and burned to the ground by AK-47-toting men on horseback known as the "Janjaweed."

Drawings are our earliest form of written communication, and, in their simplicity, they can convey difficult ideas in an instant. Where no photographic evidence exists, art can expose and document terrible crimes. Art is found in Holocaust museums because too few photographs, videos, and human survivors exist to fully describe the horrors in Nazi concentration camps. Illustrations can educate the young, inform policymakers, and shame the perpetrators. Art can propel painful discussions forward, advancing understanding and resolution.

Vannak Prum has harnessed the power of

graphic art to tell his own remarkable story. It is a story that most people could never imagine—or survive. Sold into slavery, first at sea and then on land, Prum managed to escape and return home. And now, pencil in hand, he draws us into that harrowing world of hopelessness and horror at sea. His book is both spare and devastating. Prum's message of humanity reminds us of the thousands of other men and boys around the world who still have not escaped their boats. Prum's graphic depictions are so haunting because they reveal the crushing weight of violence suffered at sea. Many of these men and boys may never make it home alive.

"My memory is a wound that will never heal."
As with many who are kidnapped, tricked, or sold into forced labor and involuntary servitude, Prum's nightmare began when he struck out to look for a job. Hoping to support his pregnant wife, Prum began his journey voluntarily. Lacking any way to earn money to support his growing family in Cambodia, Prum's desperate rural poverty and lack of education made him an easy mark for human traffickers.

Hard-hitting investigative reporting and academic studies over the last decade confirm Prum's grim illustrations of modern slavery on board fishing vessels. Modern slavery in Asia's fishing industry is both rampant and notorious. The boats operate in international waters, outside of the reach of law and monitoring. Years can pass without any opportunity to escape forced labor on the fishing vessels. And escape is not a certainty.

The sinking of the *Oyang 70*
"At about 4:40 AM on August 18, 2010, *Oyang 70*, a South Korean fishing vessel in New Zealand's exclusive economic zone, capsized and quickly sank in calm conditions with the loss of six lives," one article reported. The fishing workers killed were Indonesian, Filipino, Chinese, and Korean. The survivors told of inhumane working conditions, physical and mental abuse, and wage theft—much like Prum's experience. Christina Stringer, Glen

Simmons, and Daren Coulston, the academics who researched and wrote an exposé triggered by the sinking of the *Oyang 70*, called their study, "Not in New Zealand's Waters, Surely? Labor and Human Rights Abuses Aboard Foreign Fishing Vessels." They found that in the previous decade more than five hundred workers on fishing vessels had "jumped ship" in New Zealand to flee unbearable conditions. The researchers interviewed many of those escapees.

What emerged was a horrific picture of floating fish-processing prisons. Human life on these boats is worth less than the tons of seafood that workers pull from the ocean. The fishermen toil seven days a week, morning to night, year after year. Many do not see land for years.

There is a business model behind this fishing supply chain. In 2012, the investigative journalist E. Benjamin Skinner documented in *Businessweek* how agencies that recruit workers for international fishing ships create conditions of bonded labor—in which people desperate for work pay high fees to labor recruiters. Although the workers in New Zealand are supposed to receive a minimum wage of US$12 per hour, the reality is that bogus fees and expenses knocked their earnings down to an average of $1 an hour. Some were not paid at all. Skinner described this as "The Fishing Industry's Cruelest Catch," in which "scores of indentured workers are trawling for seafood." He interviewed companies whose opaque international supply chains mean the fish produced by slavery is shipped to restaurants and stores around the world—and, he concluded, "You may be buying it."

In 2015, the Associated Press conducted a year-long investigation, "Are slaves catching the fish you buy?", which exposed how seafood linked to forced labor was entering the supply chains of major US grocery stores. Like Prum, workers from Myanmar, Cambodia, and Laos had been sold, had their passports confiscated, and were enslaved in the fishing industry—in some cases for decades. The story led to the rescue of more than two thousand men from

Thai fishing boats operating in the Banda Sea in eastern Indonesia; the confiscation of dozens of foreign boats used for illegal fishing; and the closure of Indonesian waters to foreign fishing boats. Above all, it meant that many men returned home to relatives in Cambodia and Myanmar who had long since given up hope they would return.

What is different about Prum's first-person account is that he takes us along with him onto the boat. We meet the men who enslaved him. We see how easily people desperate to support their families can be entrapped. More important, through Prum's drawings and narrative we can empathize with people living in bondage. From the point of view of these workers, every justice system they encounter exists to protect their abusers, not to provide them with real justice. Impunity is the norm: the system does not demand accountability for the traffickers who exploit and abuse these workers.

This brings us to the policy implications of Prum's book. Trafficking, forced labor, and modern-day slavery are all crimes. These crimes are both visible and invisible. They stretch around the world—and may be as close to you as a neighbor's house or a local business. Human bondage may be present in things you buy, in the sports tournaments you watch, in the "fast fashion" clothes you wear, and in the restaurants where you eat.

In my work for Human Rights Watch, I have interviewed trafficking survivors held for years in conditions of bondage and forced labor. I once asked a survivor of forced labor working in the Washington, DC, area why she didn't just run away and report her situation to the police. She said that she didn't realize she even had rights—and she didn't think that law enforcement was there to protect her. Instead, her automatic assumption was that police were there to protect the men abusing her. As Prum's story shows, corrupt government officials and police are often paid off by the traffickers or, more shockingly, are even running trafficking networks themselves.

Bondage around the world

In 2017, the International Labor Organization, the worldwide labor standards body, worked with the Walk Free Foundation to compile new estimates of trafficking and forced labor around the globe. Those estimates indicated that in 2016 at least forty million people were held in servitude.

The fishing industry is not the only site of abuse. Construction work is yet another global industry that benefits from bonded labor. Workers who originate from poorer nations migrate or are sent to do dangerous work building skyscrapers and stadiums in wealthier nations. The North Korean government sends its workers around the globe to earn hard currency and defy increased United Nations sanctions. Some of these migrants ended up building St. Petersburg Stadium for FIFA's 2018 World Cup in Russia. It's quite clear that the Russians needed the workers to finish the stadiums but were not willing to pay fair wages and ensure safe working conditions. The losers in this arrangement were the North Korean workers who toiled and died to build a stadium while the rest of the world cheered their favorite teams, unaware.

In Qatar, which will host the soccer World Cup in 2022, two million migrant workers—95 percent of the country's population—come from Nepal and other South Asian or African countries. On the day they arrive, these migrants must surrender their passports. They quickly learn that they are now tied to their employer, under a Gulf-wide system of modern-day slavery known as *kafala*. Migrants work in perilous heat conditions—the heat is so harsh, in fact, that the World Cup tournament was rescheduled to winter to avoid endangering players and fans. In 2013, the last year for which data is available, Qatari health authorities reported 520 deaths of construction workers from Bangladesh, India, and Nepal. The deaths of workers are something sports fans should consider as they buy tickets or tune in to cheer their favorite teams. A first-person graphic account, like Prum's, that could convey such realities to an otherwise oblivious world would certainly be invaluable.

Justice out of reach?

Prum's story, told forcefully and persuasively in this graphic memoir, urges us to ask where our seafood comes from and to demand justice for the workers who have been exploited. More broadly, his story teaches us to look carefully around us, at entire industries built on supply chains that hide human bondage.

Prum's story shows that human beings who are poor and disenfranchised can unite to demand that laws, customs, and policies protect them.

Modern-day slavery affects millions around the globe, with the vast majority of people enslaved through forced labor in the private sector. With an estimated forty million people held in all forms of servitude worldwide, the US State Department estimated in 2016 that there were just 14,897 prosecutions against human traffickers in the entire world. Of those, only 1,038 were for forced labor. The remaining 13,859 cases were for sex trafficking. Experts agree that forced labor and involuntary servitude cases outnumber sex trafficking cases by a factor of three to one. But sex trafficking prosecutions outnumber forced labor prosecutions by a factor of nearly fourteen to one. States rarely summon the political will to hold traffickers in supply chains accountable.

International law mandates access to compensation and basic mental health support for trafficking victims. But prosecutors and courts worldwide continue to treat victims as criminals. Meanwhile, traffickers get away scot-free, keeping their ill-gotten gains, enjoying almost total impunity.

In fact, victims are often prosecuted for crimes they were forced to commit while being trafficked, or deported for immigration violations, as Prum was. In one large city in the US, child victims of sex trafficking participated as witnesses in a federal criminal case, while facing prostitution charges in the local juvenile court for the same acts. In the United

Kingdom, Vietnamese children forced to work in illegal marijuana greenhouses faced criminal prosecution, even after the court acknowledged them as trafficking victims. This is simply wrong. Victims should never be prosecuted for crimes they were forced to commit by their traffickers. This is particularly true for minors.

In sum, traffickers are profiting from modern slavery, and the fact that they get away with it encourages the perpetuation of their inhumane business model.

That needs to change—in Prum's homeland and yours, too. Prum's heartwrenching story clearly illustrates the experience of human trafficking, revealing the harsh reality of the hidden system that surrounds us.

I am so eager to read this book with my sons, and use it to explain the most difficult facts behind modern-day slavery. You can also share this book with policymakers, to press them to change bad laws and policies. This book should become required reading in schools, in companies, in the halls of power,

and beyond, to show not only trafficking survivors but indeed everyone that they have value, dignity, and purpose in our world.

In addition to exposing the hidden plight of forced laborers, this book can introduce readers to the modern anti-slavery movement. Like Manfred Hornung, the advocate at the Cambodian nongovernmental organization LICADHO, who helped Prum return home, there are many tenacious human rights groups and individuals who are working on the front lines to end slavery. Researchers at Human Rights Watch and Amnesty International expose abuses. Foundations like the Freedom Fund and Humanity United direct resources to anti-slavery initiatives. Hotlines and groups including Polaris and Anti-Slavery International connect victims with support. Investigative reporters like those at the Thomson Reuters Foundation, the Associated Press, and the Center for Investigative Reporting expose these abuses. And lawyers at the Human Trafficking Legal Center sue traffickers to bring justice to those whose lives and labor have been stolen.

You too can get involved and fight trafficking by reaching out to these and other local and international groups who support victims and help them rebuild their lives.

Finally, I hope the art and heart in this book will inspire the next generation of activists to put traffickers on trial and in prison, and to return the Prums of the world home to their families.

MINKY WORDEN

This book is for all the slaves in the world,
those who are free and those who are still held captive.

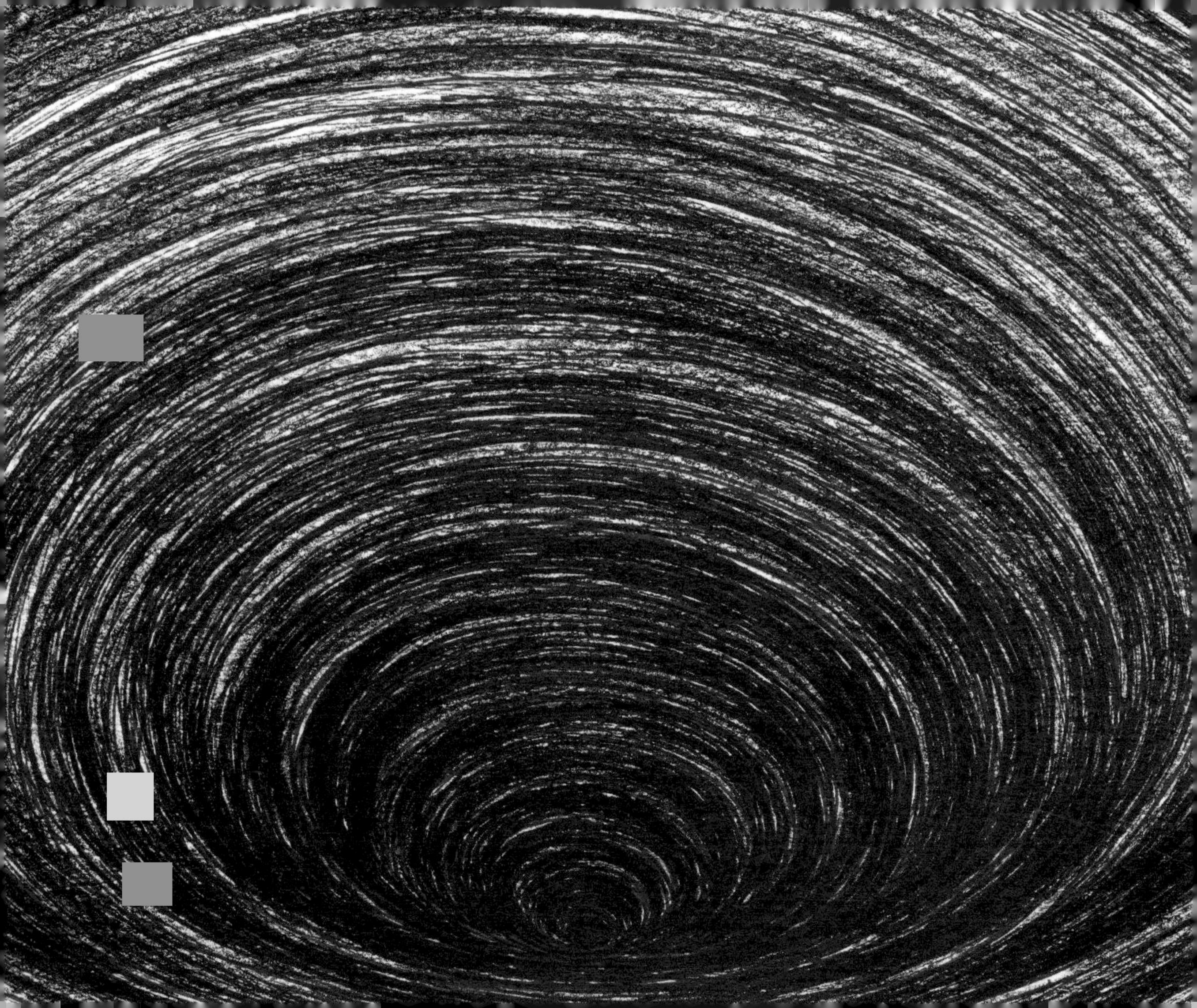

THE DEAD EYE AND THE DEEP BLUE SEA

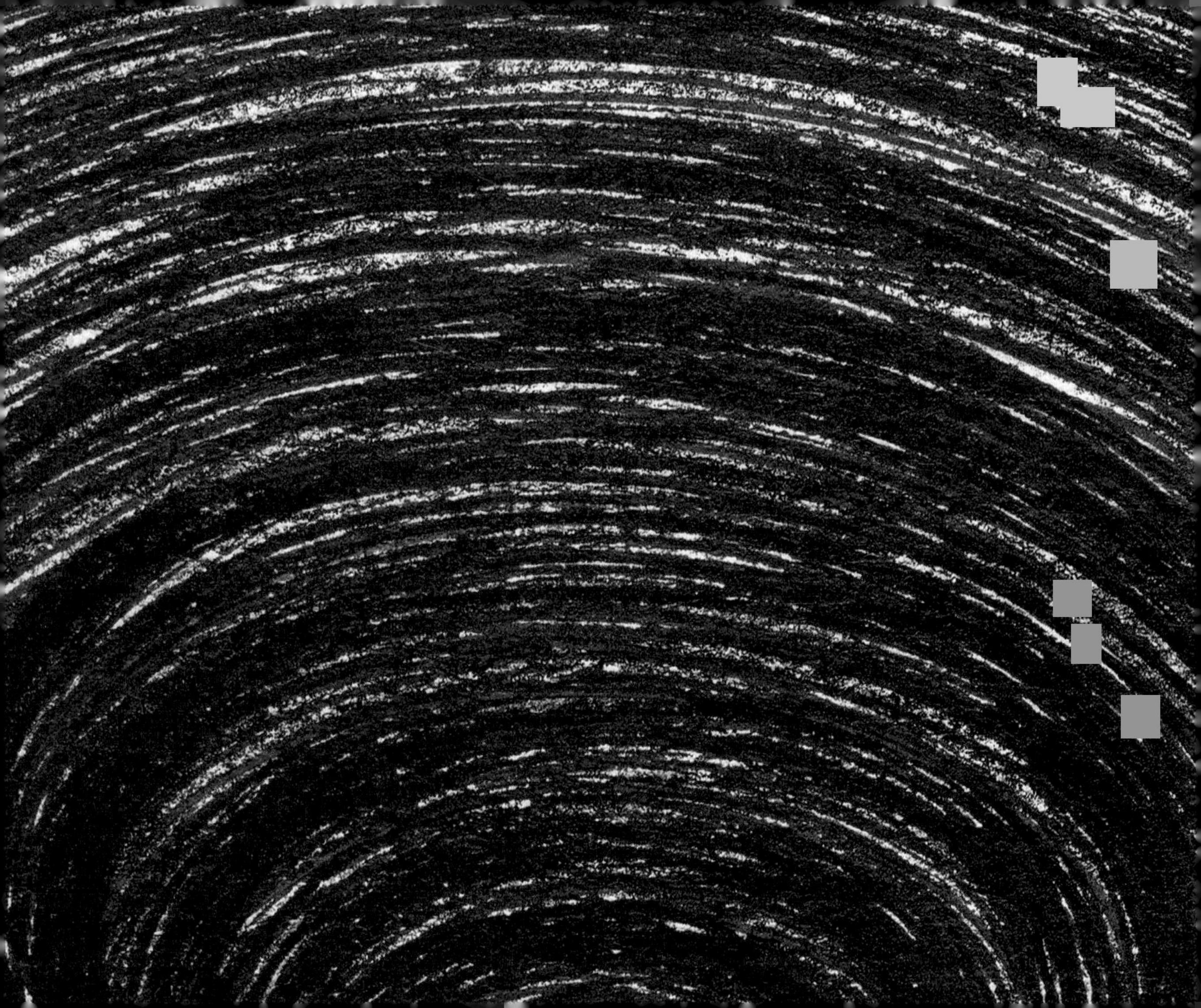

PROLOGUE

បុរេកថា
។

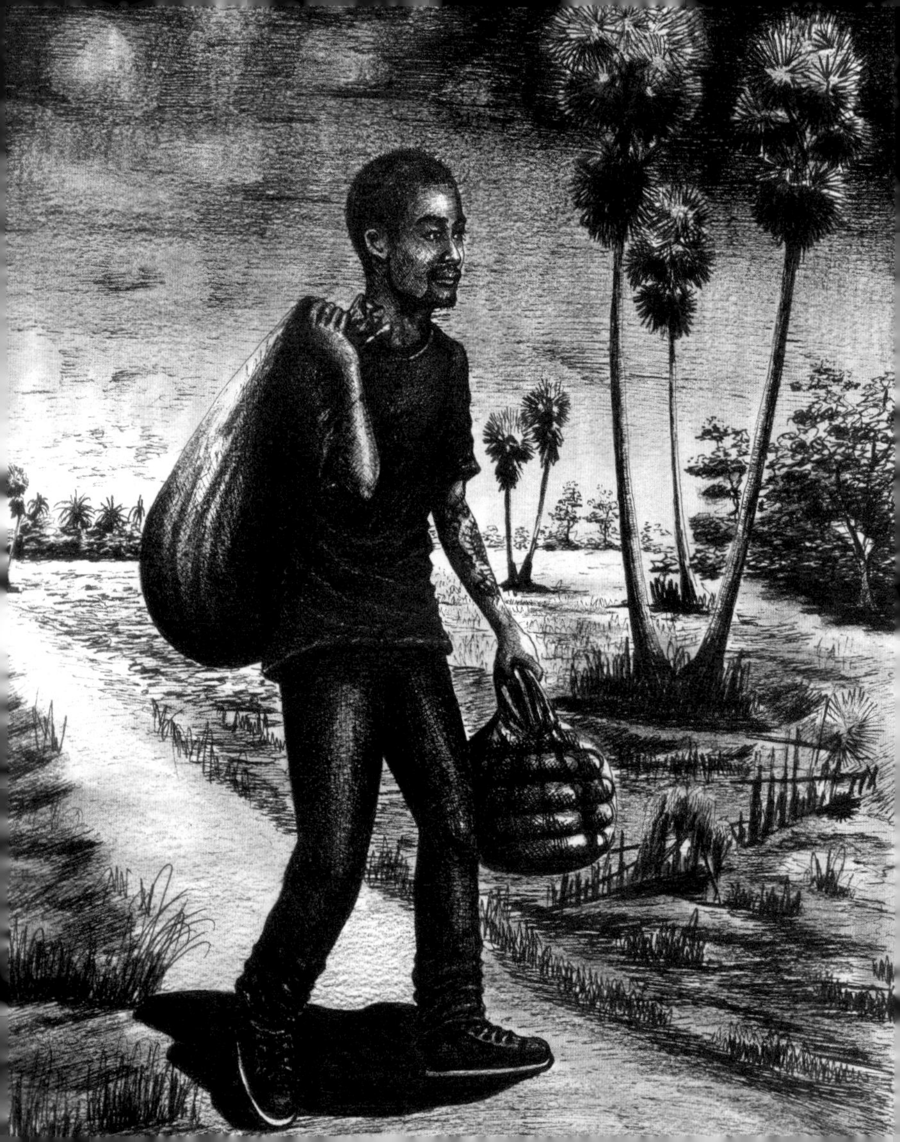

A STRANGER ENTERS THE VILLAGE. He walks slowly, looking around. He stops outside a shack and calls to a woman with a small child. She looks up, shocked.

This man is her husband, who disappeared long ago.

HE HAS CHANGED. HE'S THIN AND TANNED, WITH strange scars and tattoos on his arms. He kneels before his daughter, but the girl cries and hides in her mother's skirts. His wife comforts their daughter, then says to him, *"Just leave us alone."*

HE BEGS HER TO LISTEN. TAKING A PEN AND paper from his pocket, he shows them a terrible story. Words and pictures spill from him like water from a cracked pot: a boat, the sea, a dangerous journey. They draw closer, and look again at the strange man. That strange man is me.

DRAWING IN THE DIRT

ការគូរនៅលើដី

I'VE DRAWN ALL MY LIFE. I WAS BORN IN
1979, the second of eight children, in the year
the Khmer Rouge were defeated by Vietnam.
One of my first memories is of drawing pictures
of Bruce Lee in the dirt in front of our house.

EVERYONE WAS ALWAYS HUNGRY. WE ATE RATS AND FROGS WE CAUGHT IN THE FIELDS. THE school had no roof, so we studied in the shade of a big tree. But I rarely went to school because I had to work selling my mother's orange cakes. She promised to buy me a book full of pictures, with a photo of the whole Earth on the cover. I thought I would learn all about the world from that book. I daydreamed while I worked, flying around the world. How long would it take, I wondered. Would I ever reach the end?

THE COUNTRY WAS STILL AT WAR AND WE LIVED BETWEEN TWO
armies. Vietnamese soldiers occupied our village, and the Khmer Rouge were
everywhere, bombing towns and murdering people. Occasionally they raided
our village at night, shooting into houses, stealing our food, and terrifying people.
Once they kidnapped and killed our chief. I remember their uniforms. By then
they had stopped wearing black, and instead wore dark blue for Pol Pot.

ONE DAY I WAS DRAWING IN THE DIRT WHEN A VIETNAMESE SOLDIER STOPPED TO WATCH ME,
casting a shadow over my drawing. He didn't say anything, and after a while he went away. But later he came
back and gave me a pencil and a piece of paper, the first I had ever owned. I drew him a picture of Bruce Lee.
He liked it so much he asked my mother if he could take me back to Vietnam. She said no, of course.

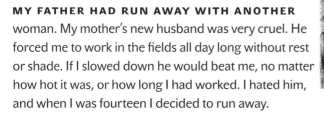

MY FATHER HAD RUN AWAY WITH ANOTHER
woman. My mother's new husband was very cruel. He
forced me to work in the fields all day long without rest
or shade. If I slowed down he would beat me, no matter
how hot it was, or how long I had worked. I hated him,
and when I was fourteen I decided to run away.

SAYING GOODBYE TO MY MOTHER WAS VERY HARD. I DIDN'T WANT TO LEAVE HER alone with that man. But I was too small to stop him. I didn't want her to worry, so I told her I was going away to study. But really I was just running away from him.

ADVENTURE

ការផ្សងព្រេង

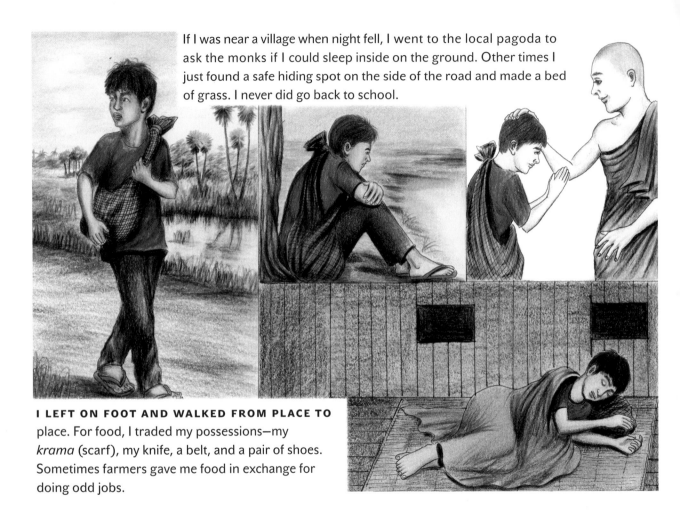

If I was near a village when night fell, I went to the local pagoda to ask the monks if I could sleep inside on the ground. Other times I just found a safe hiding spot on the side of the road and made a bed of grass. I never did go back to school.

I LEFT ON FOOT AND WALKED FROM PLACE TO place. For food, I traded my possessions—my *krama* (scarf), my knife, a belt, and a pair of shoes. Sometimes farmers gave me food in exchange for doing odd jobs.

I TRAVELED MORE THAN A HUNDRED KILOMETERS,
scrounging for food and board. Then I ran out of things
to trade. I met an army officer who said I could join his unit.
With no food or money, and no place to stay, I decided to
become a soldier. I made a plan: first I would learn how to
shoot a gun. Then I would go home and kill my stepfather.

I WAS FOURTEEN THE FIRST TIME I WENT INTO BATTLE. THERE WAS NO
training. They gave me a uniform and a gun, and sent me to fight the Khmer Rouge.
I saw men kill and be killed. I saw men and boys my age with their limbs blown
off, bleeding to death. At first I was terrified, and sure I would be next. But soon it
became as normal as watching a movie. I never shot at anyone. I aimed over their
heads. Afterward I drew what had happened and showed it to the other soldiers.

ALL THIS VIOLENCE AND DEATH BEGAN TO POISON
my mind. Day and night, I became consumed with plans
to kill my stepfather. I was filled with anger, and knew I
needed to find some peace, to wash away my sins. So I left
the army and became a monk, to learn how to release
my rage.

I ENTERED THE MONASTERY WHEN I WAS SIXTEEN.
Every day I meditated from dawn to dusk. For two years I
studied the nature of good and evil, until one day I realized
I no longer wanted to kill my stepfather. Free of my anger
and my sin, it was time for me to leave. I was just eighteen
and I wanted to see the world.

THE WAR WAS OVER, BUT THERE WAS NO WORK, SO I
rejoined the army. Instead of battles, my unit went to karaoke bars,
eating, drinking, and meeting girls. It was a lot of fun. I drew pictures,
some for the officers, but mostly for the bar girls. They loved it when
I drew their portraits, crowding around to be the next model in line.

BUT I NEVER REALLY FIT IN, AND AFTER A FEW YEARS I
took my uniform off and headed north to Angkor Wat. There
in the ruins of a Kingdom of Giants I copied carvings of ancient
battles, sketching the armies, elephants, and tigers warring on
the Great Lake. Some statues depicted the heavenly Apsara,
beautiful spirits churning the Cosmic Milk for the harvest of
Mother Rice. I copied the ancient artist to learn how to carve.
First I would draw on the stone, then hammer and chisel it
away to reveal a mystical being, or a many-headed Naga.

I GOT A JOB IN SIEM REAP, WORKING AS A SCULPTOR IN a workshop making statues to sell to rich people and tourists. We carved busts of the God King Jayavarman, Hindu spirits, and Apsara out of mountain rocks. I worked all day long, but the boss never paid me money, only enough food to survive.

MY WIFE

ប្រពន្ធខ្ញុំ

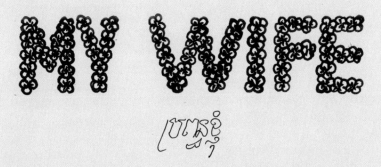

WHEN I HEARD THAT FARMERS IN BATTAMBANG
were paying for help with the harvest, I left immediately
with nothing but the clothes on my back. I arrived just in
time and was hired on the spot. It was a good year with
many crops—corn, soybeans, potatoes, sesame seeds,
and rice. People from all over the country had come for
the paid work, and we all joined together. I made good
friends in those fields as we worked side by side.

THE DEAD EYE AND THE DEEP BLUE SEA

ONE MORNING IN A FRESHLY HARVESTED FIELD, I MET
a girl called Sokun. The moment I saw her face I knew she
would be my wife. She came from another province called
Pursat. From that day on we always worked together, and we
fell in love.

WHEN THE LAST OF THE CROPS WERE HARVESTED,
Sokun agreed to marry me. We traveled to her parents'
village for their blessing. We were too poor for a proper
wedding. I had no money for a dowry. So Sokun sold her
gold earrings and we cooked food for the neighbors. We
were married in everyday clothes, in a simple ceremony with
a monk's attendant in Sokun's parents' home.

WE MOVED INTO A SMALL HUT ON HER parents' farm. I found work as a sculptor. When business was good, I brought home fifteen2 dollars a month. When it was bad, I got nothing. To get enough to eat we would scavenge in the forest for frogs, crabs, and rats. The walls of our hut were full of holes and the roof leaked when it rained. There was no well for water.

ONE DAY SOKUN SAID SHE WAS PREGNANT. I WAS GOING TO BE A FATHER, BUT HOW WOULD WE save up enough money for the hospital? We could never afford to raise and take care of our child on my sculpting. We talked and realized we had no choice. I'd have to try and find better work elsewhere.

WE PLANNED TOGETHER. THERE WERE RUMORS OF WORK IN O'UNLOK, A VILLAGE NEARBY. I would go for two months, just long enough to earn the money for Sokun's hospital stay. And then I would come home. Sokun said, *"If you don't find work, please, just come home."* But I knew I couldn't return empty-handed. Saying goodbye was very difficult. I didn't know it then, but we wouldn't see each other again for five years.

MOTO & THE MIDDLEMAN

ម៉ូតូឌុបនិង ឈ្មួញកណ្ដាល

I HITCHED A RIDE ON THE BACK OF A PICKUP
truck, but when I got to O'Unlok there was no work.
I still had no money. Then a moto driver told me, *"I
know someone who can get you work drying fish in
Thailand. There's lots of work over there, and the
pay is good."* I was confused about what I should do.

A FRIEND OF MINE FROM THE HARVEST DAYS, Rus, lived nearby. We were like brothers, so I asked the moto driver to take me to him. Rus had also been unable to find work. He thought that Thailand sounded like a good idea, but I was unsure. The moto driver said, *"Brother, are you in or not?"*

IT SOUNDED TOO GOOD TO BE TRUE, LIKE A TRICK. BUT ALL I HAD WAS 10,000 RIEL (ABOUT $2.50 USD) in my pocket: too little to go on, and not enough to go back. The driver said, *"Don't worry about the money. The middleman will pay me when you arrive."* So I decided to go, and was surprised when Rus decided to come along, too. On the way there we passed trucks full of people heading for the border. They all looked like us, poor and worried.

THE MIDDLEMAN'S HOUSE WAS IN MALAI, A TOWN ON THE THAI BORDER. THERE WAS NO work there either. When I tried to leave, the middleman said, *"You are free to go, but you'll need to repay your travel costs first."* I didn't have enough money. Now I was scared. I gave him my money to be changed into Thai baht, but he never gave it back. So I had nothing. They led us to a wooden house and told us all to wait there.

THE DEAD EYE AND THE DEEP BLUE SEA

THERE WERE ABOUT TWENTY PEOPLE
there, men, women, and even a few children, all
waiting to cross. The middleman warned us to
be quiet and stay out of sight. He said that Thai
border soldiers had killed people trying to cross.

THE DEAD EYE AND THE DEEP BLUE SEA

CROSSING THE BORDER

ಮಿಸ ಬಾರ್ಡರ

WE HID THERE FOR A FEW
days, then one night it started
to rain. As the storm gathered
strength, the middleman gave the
orders for us to cross. Our guide
said, *"Be totally silent and you
won't be shot."* We filed through
the darkness, mute, with lightning
crackling over our heads. At a canal
we waded through water up to our
necks, and lifted the children who
couldn't reach the surface.

FINALLY WE REACHED A ROAD AND TWO WAITING PICKUP TRUCKS. THE GUIDES MADE US LIE down on top of each other in the back, three people deep, four sideways, and three across. They told us to leave breathing spaces. I was put on the bottom layer. They covered us with a black tarp, and the car began to move. Arms and legs fell on top of me. The smell was overpowering. I felt that I was suffocating. We drove for two hours, to a farm somewhere near a city.

WE STAYED FOR SEVERAL DAYS, AND THEY ONLY FED US ONCE
a day. New people were always arriving. Some had paid money, others
had not. After a couple of days there were more than a hundred people being
kept in small farm huts. Some had suitcases, but no one had passports or
documents. Rus and I had nothing but the clothes on our backs.

ONE DAY A MAN WE HAD CROSSED THE BORDER WITH whispered in my ear, *"You guys are being watched. I heard the middleman tell the workers to take special care of you and guard you carefully."*

THE DEAD EYE AND THE DEEP BLUE SEA

43

WE WERE SCARED. RUS WANTED TO MAKE A RUN FOR IT IMMEDIATELY.
I thought that we should stay. We knew nothing about Thailand. If soldiers caught
us, we might be killed. I convinced Rus to lay low and we didn't try to escape.

THE WRITING ON THE WALL

ការសរសេរអក្សរនៅលើជញ្ជាំង

THE NEXT NIGHT THEY LOADED EVERYONE INTO A CONVOY OF CARS. AFTER A SHORT DRIVE A tattooed man standing in the middle of the road waved us down. He read our names off one by one, dividing us into smaller groups. Rus and I noticed that everyone in our group was a man, and that no one had paid anything to get here. It seemed strange.

THE PROCESS TOOK A LONG TIME
and it was nearly dawn when we were
all loaded into taxis, four people per car.

AS THE SUN ROSE OUR TAXI PULLED UP TO A DILAPIDATED BUILDING. WE WERE ORDERED INTO a room with no furniture and locked inside. We were all Khmer men, and I was the oldest. Outside we could hear the sounds of the sea. Peeking through a hole, I saw countless boats tied to a wharf. We knocked on the door to tell the guards we were hungry and they gave us a small meal of rice and pork, some cigarettes, and whiskey. We talked only a little, wondering what would become of us.

THE WALLS WERE COVERED IN MESSAGES LEFT by men gone before me. One I could read clearly said, *"Don't let the sun go down on us."* I decided to leave my own message: *"If fate is kind we will meet one day."* Underneath I wrote a name, *"Baknam Konkea,"* Ocean's End: the name for my unborn child.

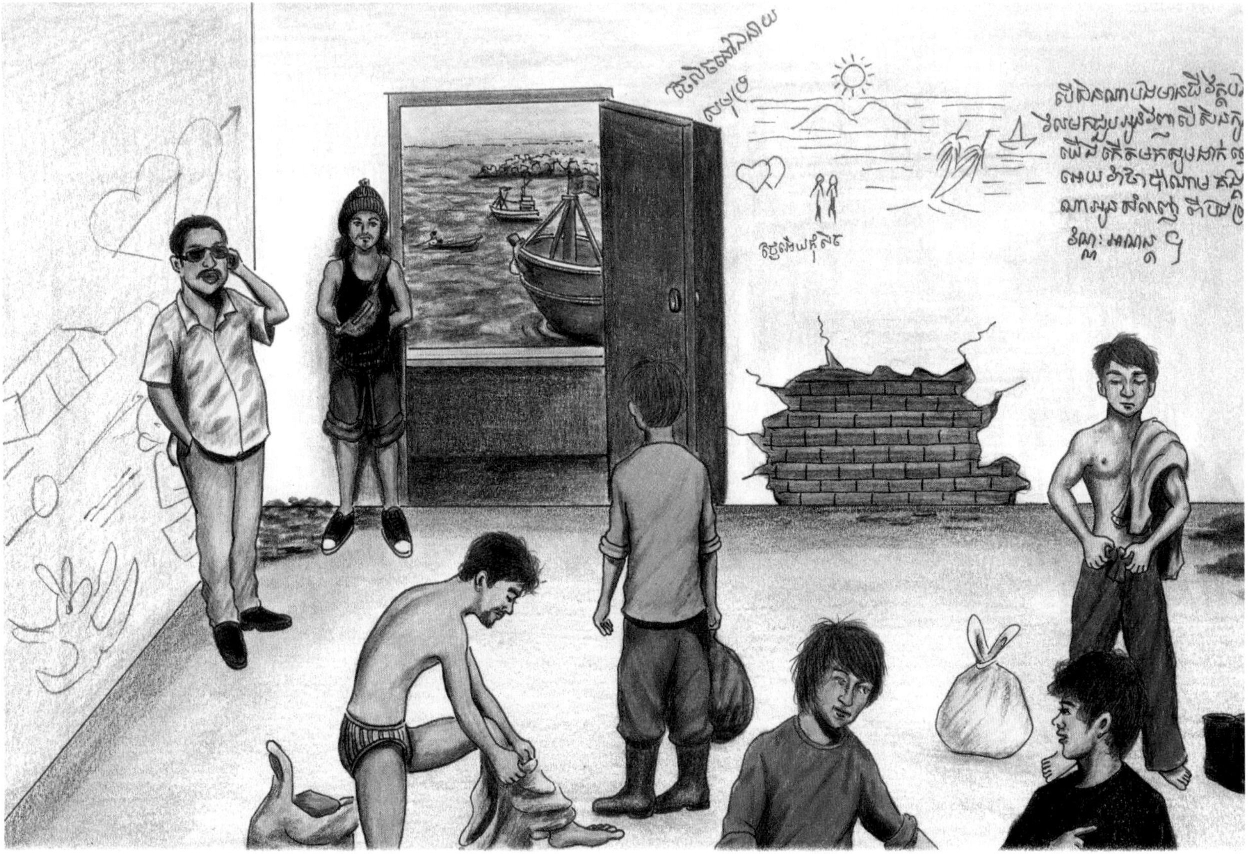

THE SUN WAS HIGH WHEN THE DOOR OPENED AND THE BOSS WALKED IN. HE MADE US LINE UP and walked along squeezing our muscles and pulling our eyelids. When he was satisfied, they handed out work clothes: shirts, fishing pants, and rubber boots. Then the door was locked again for another hungry night.

THE TOOK THO

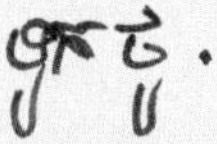

THE NEXT MORNING THEY OPENED THE door and led us to the boats. There were nine Cambodians and three Khmer Surin from Thailand. Climbing aboard a big ship, they made us lie down behind the gunnel to hide from the police. All the while Rus kept saying, *"Why didn't we run when we had the chance?"* There was no hope of escape now. I accepted my fate.

THE DEAD EYE AND THE DEEP BLUE SEA

THE BOAT CAST OFF AND ITS HUGE ENGINES ROARED AS WE PULLED OUT OF THE HARBOR. WE
had to hide for about an hour before we could get up. Then we were allowed to move around and speak
with the crew. They all said that they had been aboard the ship for years. None of them knew the fate of their
families. In time these men would become my friends. They told us this was the *took tho,* the supply ship that
serviced the fishing fleet. It carried us out on the far, wide sea.

I ASKED A CAMBODIAN MAN WHEN I WOULD go home. He answered with a question, *"Did you pay to get here?"* I said no, and he said, *"Well, stop asking questions. You have been sold."*

THE DEAD EYE AND THE DEEP BLUE SEA

THE OLD MAN

WE WERE OUT TO sea for days when an older man sat down next to me and asked for a cigarette. As we smoked he asked, *"If I have been sold, what will my children do?"* He didn't sound angry, but shocked, like a man who has lost his soul. *"What will they eat,"* he asked, *"and how will they survive?"* His story was like mine, and we both began to weep. He stood up and started pacing back and forth.

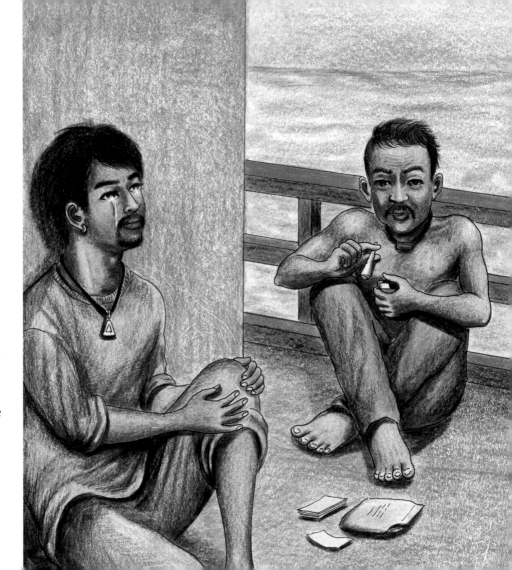

UP AND DOWN, ALL DAY HE PACED THE
decks, muttering to himself. The next morning
I saw him standing in the ship's bow. He looked
like he was brooding, deep in thought. Then
without warning he jumped. I screamed, *"Man
overboard!"* and started running. *"Stop the boat!"*

THE BOAT TURNED AROUND AND
everyone rushed to the bow to help him.
The crew and I fished him out of the sea.
He was limp and hardly breathing. I pushed
on his stomach and he threw up seawater.

SUDDENLY THE CAPTAIN APPEARED AND SHOUTED at us, *"Throw him back!"* Everybody froze. I couldn't believe what I was hearing. The first mate growled, *"Do you want to live? Do it! The sea gods have already taken him. Don't make them angry. Throw him back in."* Incredibly, four crewmen picked him up. He was too weak to struggle. And they threw him into the sea.

THE DEAD EYE AND THE DEEP BLUE SEA

59

HE HIT THE WATER AND POPPED UP AGAIN. THEN THE
boat's wake swamped him. He fell behind us, waving frantically
and screaming for help. I took off my shirt and threw it in, and
my cigarettes and lighter, so he would have something to smoke in the afterlife. I watched as waves washed
over him. I watched him appear and disappear, appear and disappear, and finally disappear.

THE TOOR OH

THE NEXT DAY WE MET UP WITH thirty smaller fishing trawlers. This was the fishing fleet. These boats we called *took oh*. They were smaller than the *took tho* and were always at sea, never returning to port. Rus and I were assigned to the same boat. It was blue, about twenty meters long and six meters wide. Because we were in Malaysian waters, it was flying a Malaysian flag. We had a complete set of flags, one for each country.

GETTING ABOARD WAS VERY
dangerous. We had to leap across the gap
between the two moving ships. I waited
until the swell lifted the two huge hulls
together and jumped onto my new home.

NONE OF THE MEN ON BOARD LOOKED
friendly. They were from everywhere—Laos, Burma,
Thailand, and Cambodia. All were muscly, with long,
wild hair, and they were covered in tattoos. I walked
gently and tried not to make eye contact. When they
asked us if we wanted a rest, I said no. I thought if I
worked harder they might let me go home.

ONE OF THE CAMBODIANS NODDED TO
me as I walked past, so I asked him, *"How long have you been here?"* He smiled and said, *"Oh, eight years, but I will be going home any day now."* He was a slave like me.

WE LEARNED THE JOB AS FAST AS WE could. The orders were all in Thai so I just copied everyone else. We would haul the nets out of the sea and sort the catch, day and night. It was exhausting. But I listened hard and did what I was told. Soon I could understand Thai.

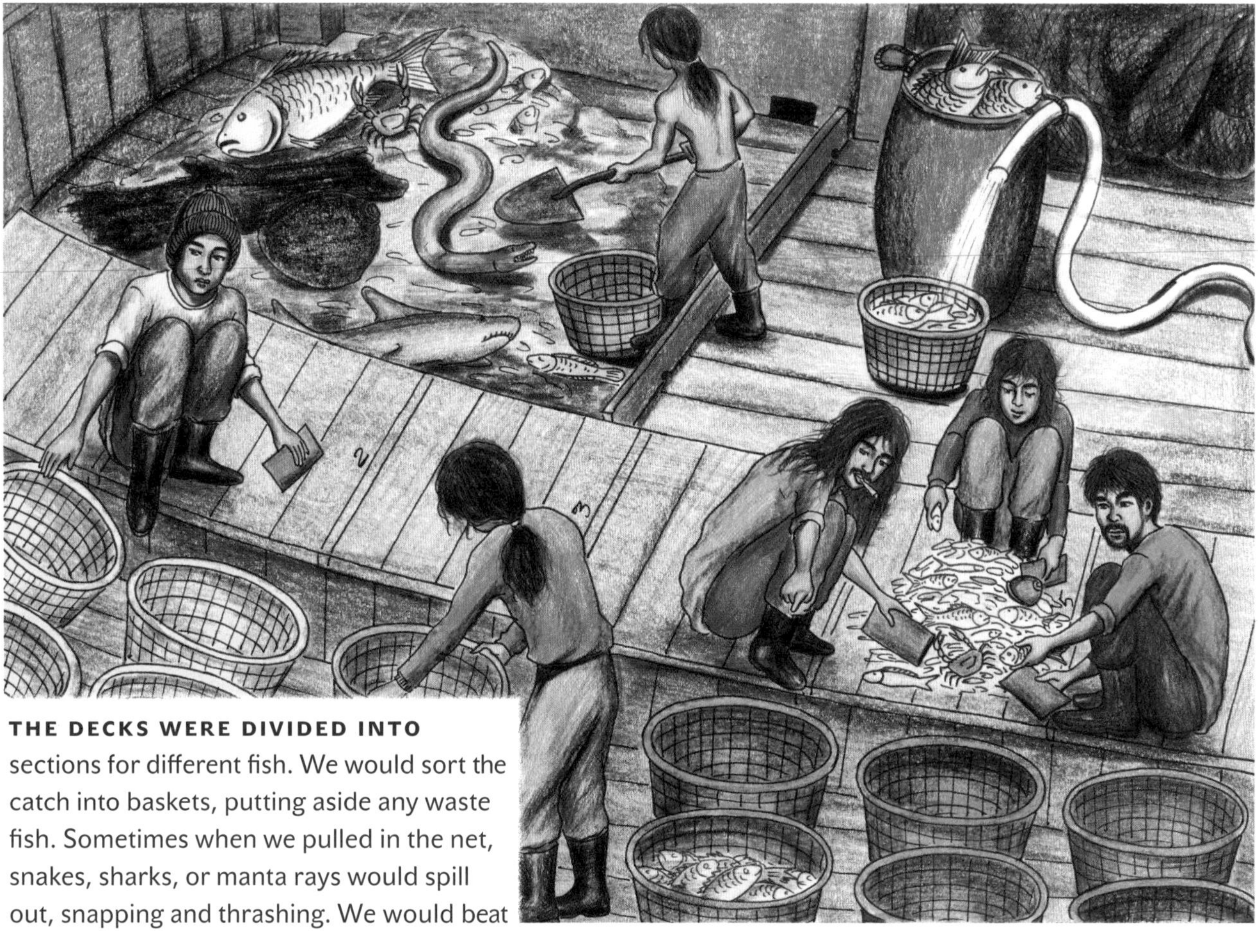

THE DECKS WERE DIVIDED INTO sections for different fish. We would sort the catch into baskets, putting aside any waste fish. Sometimes when we pulled in the net, snakes, sharks, or manta rays would spill out, snapping and thrashing. We would beat them with shovels until they were dead.

THERE WERE TWENTY OR MORE kinds of fish, big and small. When they were sorted into baskets we lowered them into the ice room under the decks.

THE DEAD EYE AND THE DEEP BLUE SEA

HONG LERK, **THE FREEZER ROOM,**
was kept cold with ice from the supply ship,
and was used to store the catch. It was a
dangerous place, very slippery, with heavy
loads. People could get killed down there.

ONCE A MONTH THE *TOOK THO* CAME TO COLLECT the fish. Offloading would take a full day and night. And as soon as we finished we would be forced to set the nets and start all over again. So the work continued, day in and day out, month after month.

ALL OF THE WASTE FISH, CRABS, SNAKES, AND
anything they couldn't sell was thrown into the bottom
of the hold. There it was left to rot for months, releasing
a gas called *brakai* that smelled so strong it nearly
made me faint. *Brakai* was used in gas stoves but was
poisonous and its fumes could kill you.

THE DEAD EYE AND THE DEEP BLUE SEA

71

OUR ORDERS CAME FROM THE FIRST MATE,
hou na. He would enforce the captain's commands. Our
hou na was a Thai who treated us like animals. He beat
the slow and the weak. He made a knife from the poison
barb of a stingray's tail and would threaten to kill us with
it if we reacted too slowly or tried to rest.

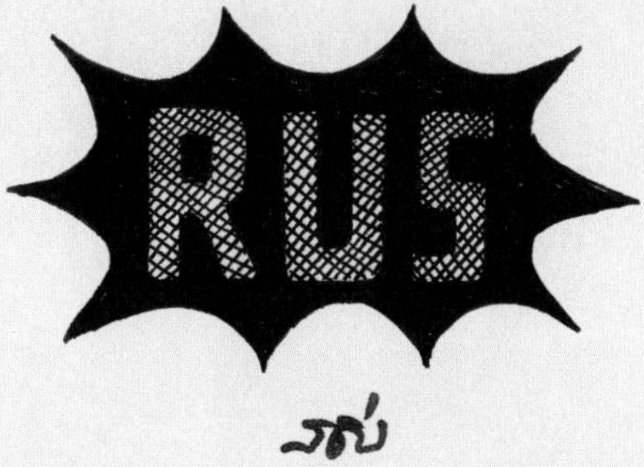
RUS

NOT LONG AFTER WE HAD offloaded the first month's catch, Rus got sick. He lost all his strength and couldn't work. When the *hou na* saw him taking a rest he screamed at him, *"What do you think you are doing? Get back to work before I beat you to a bloody pulp!"*

RUS STUMBLED BACK TO WORK, BUT ABOUT AN HOUR
later he was overcome by fever and hunger, and snuck back to the
stern to cook a fish. One Khmer man called Yourng, who had been
on the boat for years, saw Rus and followed him. Yourng grabbed
Rus and yelled, *"What the fuck do you think you are doing?"*

I HEARD THE COMMOTION AND HURRIED TO help Rus. When Yourng saw me coming he tried to hit me with a big hammer. This made me mad and I started to fight. I asked Rus to help, but he was too weak. Finally I pinned Yourng down on the deck and yelled in his face, *"Have you had enough? Do you want more?"*

I LET HIM GO BUT HE CAME STRAIGHT BACK AT me. By now the others were crowding around, telling him to calm down. Yourng stopped and walked away. Rus was growing sicker by the minute and I was scared. If I'd listened to him back in Thailand, we wouldn't even be here.

I WENT TO SEE THE CAPTAIN AT THE HELM OF THE BOAT AND BEGGED HIM TO LET RUS GO home. He said no without bothering to look up at me. I went back to Rus and promised him, *"I won't give up. I was the one that got us here, and I will get us out. I'm going to talk to the boss again."*

LATER THAT WEEK AS WE WERE HAULING in the nets, a rope got snagged and snapped with a crack like a gunshot. It hit Rus's hand, breaking several bones. It also hit Yourng, slashing his face, opening a deep cut, and knocking him out.

THE DEAD EYE AND THE DEEP BLUE SEA

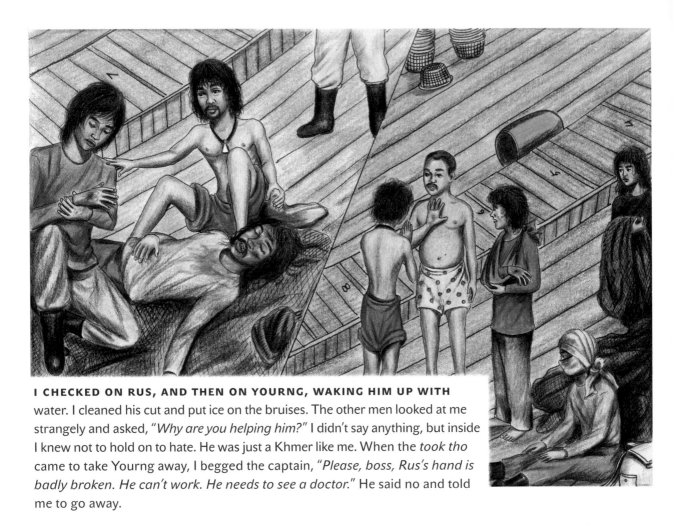

I CHECKED ON RUS, AND THEN ON YOURNG, WAKING HIM UP WITH
water. I cleaned his cut and put ice on the bruises. The other men looked at me
strangely and asked, *"Why are you helping him?"* I didn't say anything, but inside
I knew not to hold on to hate. He was just a Khmer like me. When the *took tho*
came to take Yourng away, I begged the captain, *"Please, boss, Rus's hand is
badly broken. He can't work. He needs to see a doctor."* He said no and told
me to go away.

I WHISPERED TO RUS, *"GET READY. I'LL TELL YOU WHEN."* **WHEN** Yourng was aboard and the boats were being untied, I pushed Rus forward, saying, *"Quick, jump. I'll deal with the boss. Go!"* He landed on the other boat and looked back at me. I looked at the boss for a moment. Then I went back to work as if nothing had happened. I felt the boss staring at me for a moment. Then he walked away. He never mentioned it. Rus went home. But my journey was just beginning.

THE DEAD EYE AND THE DEEP BLUE SEA

LIFE ON THE BOAT

ជីវិតនៅលើទូក

THE BOAT WAS SMALL, BUT IT became my whole world. I was one of the smallest on board, but I became stronger, my muscles got hard, and my hair grew down to my shoulders.

Everything we had came from the *took tho* or the sea. We had no money, so we collected seahorses. The Chinese dry and eat them to strengthen their bones. We traded them for cigarettes, alcohol, and drugs with the men on the *took tho*.

I CAUGHT SEAHORSES IN THE NETS FOR months until I had saved up a kilo of them. On land this was worth 10,000 baht (or $300 USD). One of the men on the *took tho* agreed to get me a camera. As he gave it to me he said, *"Be careful, brother. Make sure no one ever sees it."* Secretly I took photos. I hoped one day to show the world what happens far out at sea.

THE WORK WAS EXHAUSTING AND NEVER ended. We slept for three hours a night and ate two meals of cold rice a day. But we always had plenty of coffee and cigarettes. We drank coffee by the liter and smoked constantly to stay awake. Some men also took *ya maa,** which means *madness drug.* The *took tho* men traded their drugs for dried seahorses.

*Yaba, ya ba, ya maa: a combination of methamphetamine and caffeine, taken as tablets, cooked and inhaled, or ground up and snorted or injected.

THE DEAD EYE AND THE DEEP BLUE SEA

THEY SAID, *"IT GIVES YOU EXTRA STRENGTH,"* AND OFFERED TO GIVE ME SOME to try for free. At first it was great. I had more energy and didn't need to sleep. But after a few days all my strength drained away. I lost my appetite and couldn't sleep. I decided never to use it again. In the years since, I've seen other men ruined by their addictions, exhausted, sleepless, and in a waking nightmare. Others fall silent and never speak again. It is a cruel death.

WE WERE ALLOWED TO WASH EVERY DAY AFTER WORK,
first in seawater, then in fresh water. Fresh water was precious and
all ten of us shared a single bucket. If we took more, the *hou na*
would beat us. If we spilled it, we were scolded like dogs. Fights
often broke out at bath time, especially if anyone grabbed another
man's clothes.

FIGHTS HAPPENED ALL THE TIME, EVEN JUST FOR
fun. A man who used to be a Thai soldier challenged
me. We'd fight late into the night, and then start again
in the morning. If I lost focus he would beat me. But
eventually I wore him down until he surrendered, and
we became friends.

THE DEAD EYE AND THE DEEP BLUE SEA

THE *HOU NA* WAS ALWAYS ANGRY. ONCE A MAN CALLED
Chet got sick and took some extra rice for strength. The *hou na*
saw this and said, *"Hey, Chet, you can't work, but you sure can eat!
I should feed you to the fish."* He got so worked up it looked like he
would kill Chet. I calmed him down, but he never let up. If we were
exhausted he would beat us to make us work even harder.

Fishing slave
—VANNAK ANAN PRUM
05/06/2006

THE DEADLIEST JOB

ការងារដែលមានគ្រោះថ្នាក់បំផុត

THE SEA WAS SO BIG. MEN ON OTHER BOATS
often talked about catching corpses in the nets. At
first I didn't believe them. Then one day a headless
body fell out of our nets. The body was half-eaten,
as if the ocean hadn't finished devouring it yet.

STRANGE RUMORS PASSED AROUND THE FLEET. MEN
reported seeing real monsters, giant octopuses longer than the
boats, massive sea snakes, and ships sunk by whales. I heard of a
man who was going to the toilet and was dragged under the waves
by a giant octopus. I never saw these creatures, but I know they exist.

THE DEAD EYE AND THE DEEP BLUE SEA

THE GREATEST THREAT WAS THE BOAT ITSELF. SNAPPING CABLES, CAGES AND CONTAINERS sliding around on the deck, the ship lurching in a swell. Splinters and broken bones, and men knocked unconscious. Once a man's foot got tangled in the net as it was being dropped into the sea and he was dragged overboard. Men died this way, their necks broken, dead by the time they were pulled aboard.

EVEN TAKING A SHIT WAS DANGEROUS. WE USED A
rope harness to hang over the stern. One night I nearly died
doing this when the rope broke and I barely caught myself from
falling in. Another time a shark leapt out of the water trying to bite
my ass. It just missed me. A bathroom break could turn deadly.

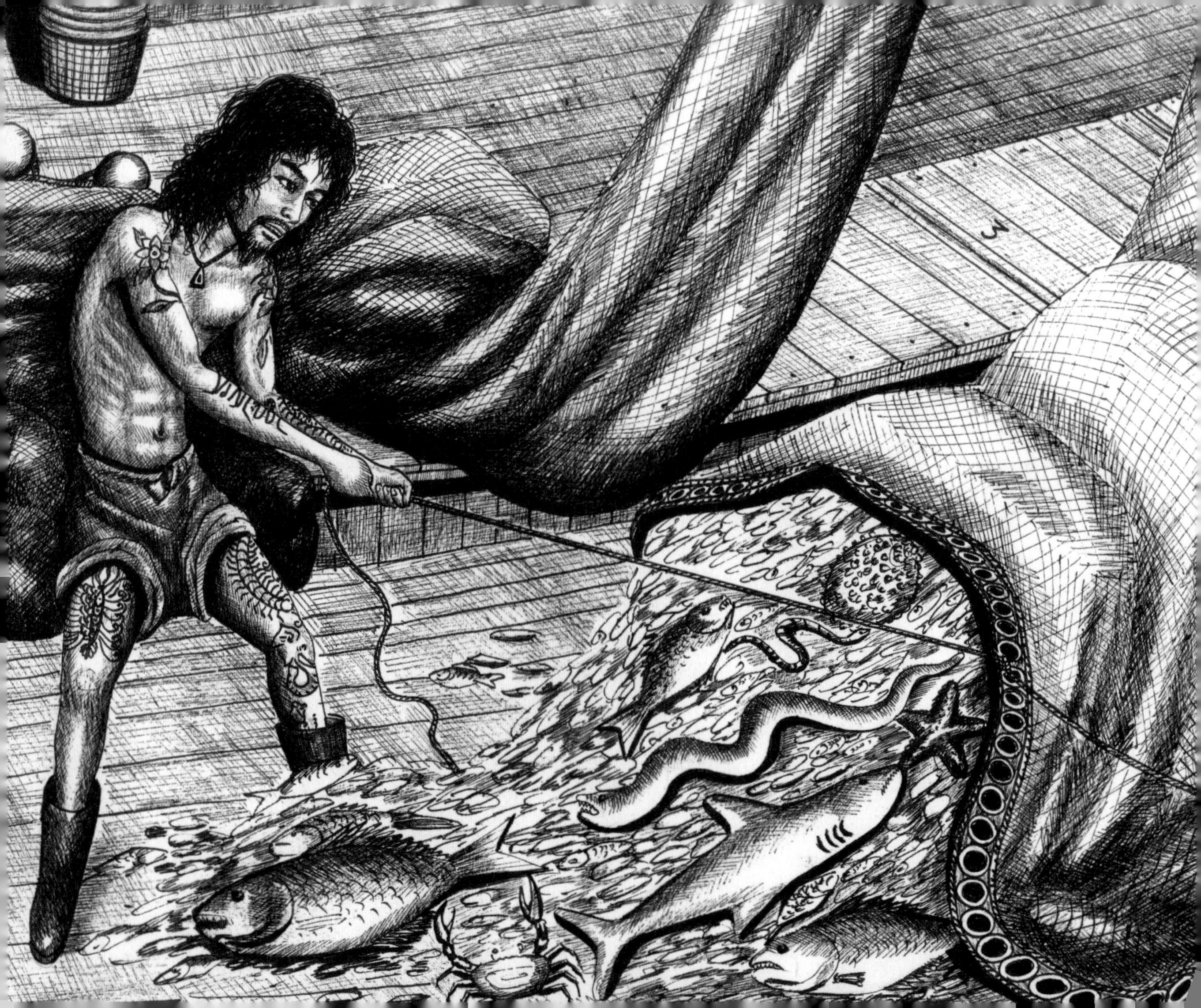

WRITING ON THE SKIN

សាក់លើស្បែក

MONTHS TURNED INTO YEARS. I GREW TIRED IN MY HEART AND MIND. I THOUGHT ABOUT MY
wife and my child all the time. How would I survive? How would I ever get home again? I tried to find ways to
make friends, to escape the fights and beatings. Then I realized everybody had tattoos. I found a good piece
of wood and whittled a long, slender stick.

I STRAIGHTENED A FISHING HOOK
and fixed it to the end of the stick. This
would be my needle. But what could I
use for ink? I scraped black soot from the
boat's chimney and mixed it with water,
adding toothpaste to make it clean.

I PRACTICED ON MY OWN LEG WHEN I WAS alone, and I wore pants to hide its progress. It took a few nights, but soon I had tattooed a black centipede on my thigh. When it was ready, I rolled up my pants so the others could see. They were surprised and couldn't believe I'd done it myself.

OTHER MEN STARTED TO ASK ME TO DO TATTOOS FOR
them. I tattooed an immense tiger across one man's back. Word
spread to other boats. I became famous. The men in the fleet
called me *acharn sut,* tattoo teacher. I did hundreds of tattoos
on men from many countries. It helped keep me safe from
some of the violence.

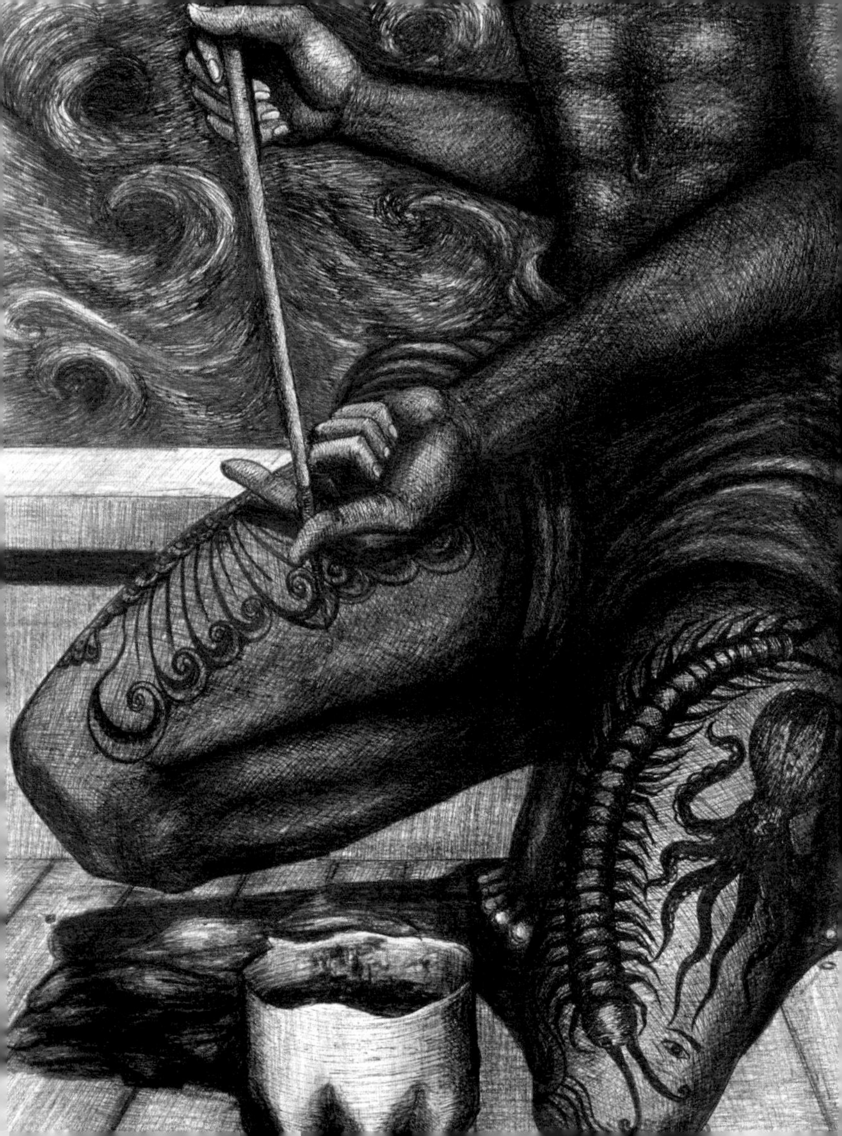

FIRE AT SEA

TIME PASSED AND I SURVIVED. ONE DAY WE WERE FISHING ILLEGALLY IN INDONESIAN WATERS, flying the Indonesian flag. We saw a navy ship on the horizon. It was heading our way fast. So we started frantically hauling the nets up out of the water. But the captain stopped us and instead cut all the lines. He ordered us below and set the autopilot toward international waters.

AS SOON AS THEY GOT CLOSE, THE NAVY SHIP OPENED fire. They pulled alongside us and threw Molotov cocktails onto our decks. They were trying to sink us. I was worried about the gas bottles on the deck. If they caught fire the whole ship would explode. I ran upstairs to douse the flames.

THE MEN ON THE NAVY SHIP SHOT AT ME. I CRAWLED
along the gunwale and bullets splintered the wood around me.
I retreated back below deck, and for ten hours we hid in the
hold thick with fumes. The engine shuddered next to us in the
darkness, and the navy ship followed with fire, machine guns,
and water cannons.

EVENTUALLY WE DRIFTED INTO MALAYSIAN waters. The Indonesians stopped and watched us go. We were alive, but the boat was destroyed and rapidly taking on water. We spent all night bailing out the ship, and the next day, and the next.

WE DRIFTED FOR A WEEK BEFORE THE *took tho* rescued us. They split us up onto different boats. The boat I was on turned toward Malaysia. I was one step further away from home, with nothing left to do but survive.

THE DEAD EYE AND THE DEEP BLUE SEA

THE NEW BOAT

A NEW BOAT MEANT A NEW BOSS, NEW *HOU NA,* and a new crew. I didn't know anyone. The *hou na* had a cruel face. Some ships' captains were worse than others. But they always treated newcomers harshly. I knew that I'd have to work harder than ever before.

THE *HOU NA* PROWLED THE DECK, SHOUTING HIS ORDERS. THE CAPTAIN STEERED FROM HIS quarters in the stern, with computers and navigation equipment. He never talked to us directly, but would shout insults into his microphone as we worked: *"Hey, you, motherfucker, you're an animal, you're a buffalo! Crazy dog. Moron. You stupid fuck!"* It made us nervous, and sometimes we made mistakes, and then we got beaten.

THIS CAPTAIN HAD A WHIP MADE FROM THE tail of a manta ray. It was as thick as your big toe. If you didn't move fast enough he'd use his whip. It made deep cuts and bruises right inside your body. Getting hit by the captain's whip left an injury that would last a lifetime.

THE DEAD EYE AND THE DEEP BLUE SEA

TWO GUYS

บุษบาลีลัก

I BEGAN TO FIND MY PLACE AND
got to know the other men. There
were two Thai who were best
friends, Kay and Dam. Kay was
popular with everyone. They had
paid to work, so they were treated
better than the rest of us, who'd
been sold. They made lots of money
and they took lots of drugs, mostly
sniffing glue.

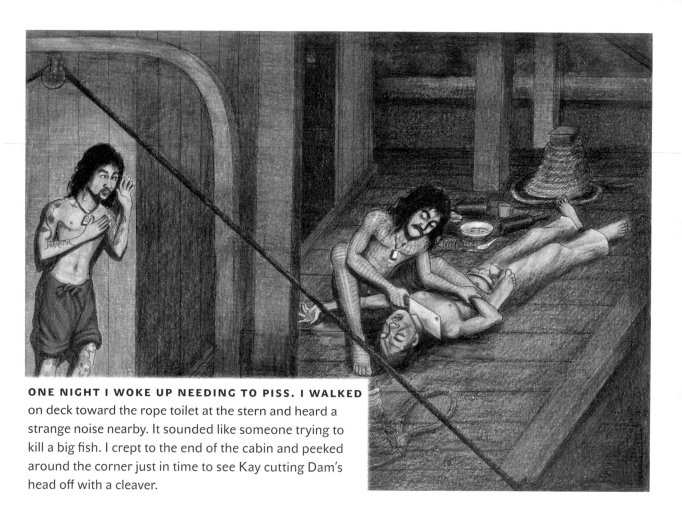

ONE NIGHT I WOKE UP NEEDING TO PISS. I WALKED on deck toward the rope toilet at the stern and heard a strange noise nearby. It sounded like someone trying to kill a big fish. I crept to the end of the cabin and peeked around the corner just in time to see Kay cutting Dam's head off with a cleaver.

KAY PICKED UP DAM'S HEADLESS CORPSE, AND
threw it over the stern into the sea, followed by the head.
I didn't stay to watch. I hurried back to the cabin and lay
quietly between the sleeping men. After a while I heard
Kay's footsteps and then just the sound of the engine in
the darkness.

116

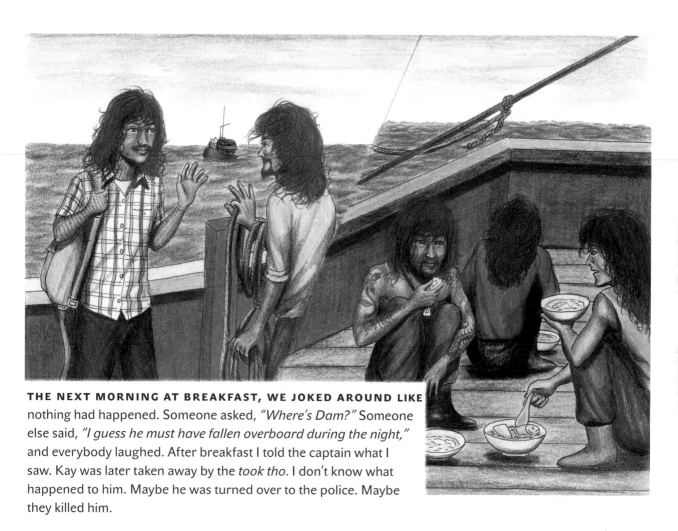

THE NEXT MORNING AT BREAKFAST, WE JOKED AROUND LIKE nothing had happened. Someone asked, *"Where's Dam?"* Someone else said, *"I guess he must have fallen overboard during the night,"* and everybody laughed. After breakfast I told the captain what I saw. Kay was later taken away by the *took tho*. I don't know what happened to him. Maybe he was turned over to the police. Maybe they killed him.

THE DEAD EYE AND THE DEEP BLUE SEA 117

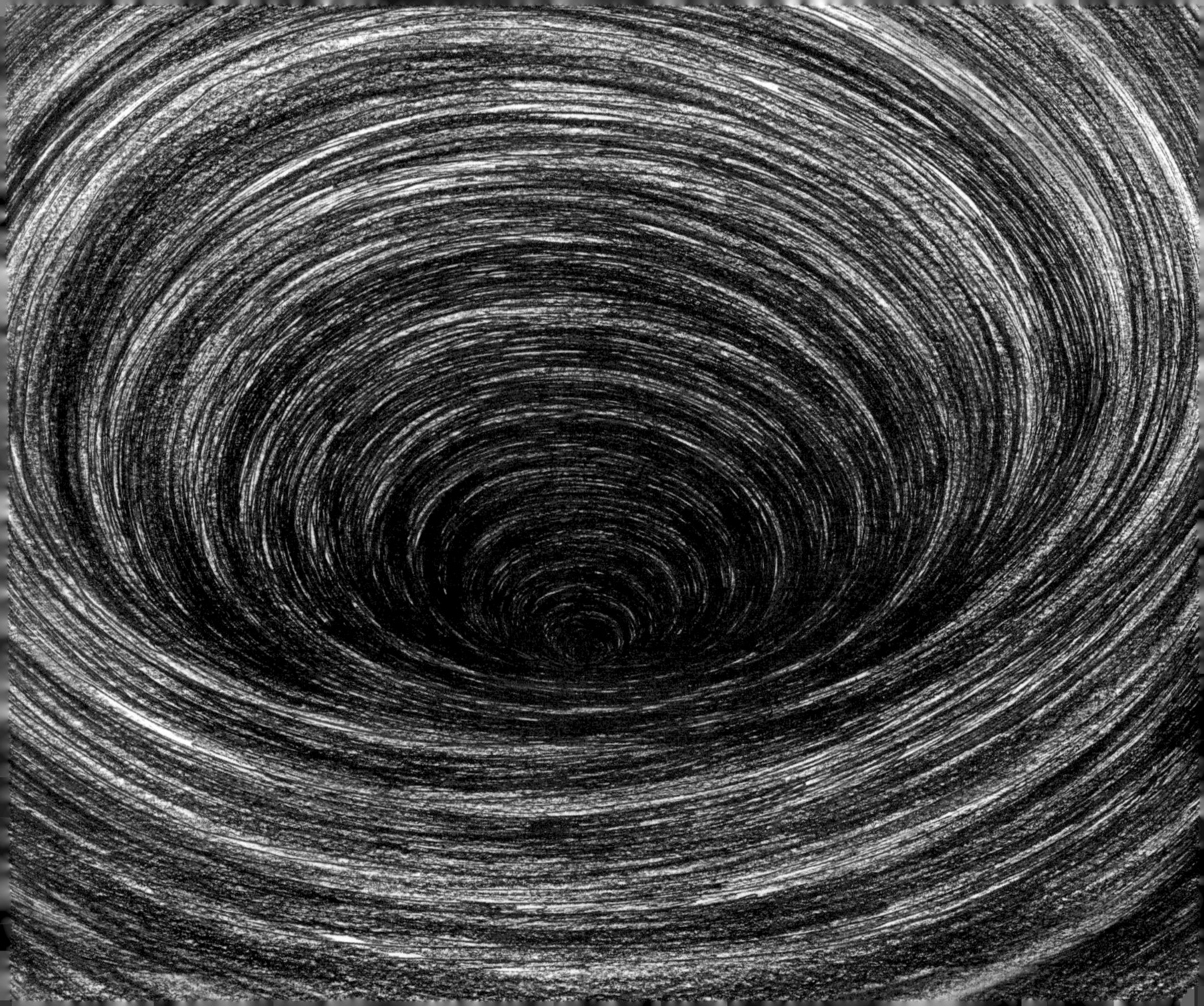

MY FRIEND K'NACK

បេក្ខជ្រ របស់ខ្ញុំ ឃ្នាក់

THE ONLY WOMAN in the fleet was on our boat. K'nack was a Cambodian lady boy who took care of the captain. She was beautiful and kind, with long hair and a round face. The whole fleet was in love with her. No one would ever have touched her or talked badly to her. Whenever she walked by, we worked extra hard to show how strong we were. Most of the men thought she really was a woman. She was the only woman we had.

K'NACK WOULD TEASE ME. SHE GAVE ME CIGARETTES AND coffee. People said we were in love, but I never touched her. Once I asked her to escape with me, but she said, *"No one sold me. I work here because I want to help my family."* I drew her picture, and when I gave it to her she was really surprised. It made her so happy.

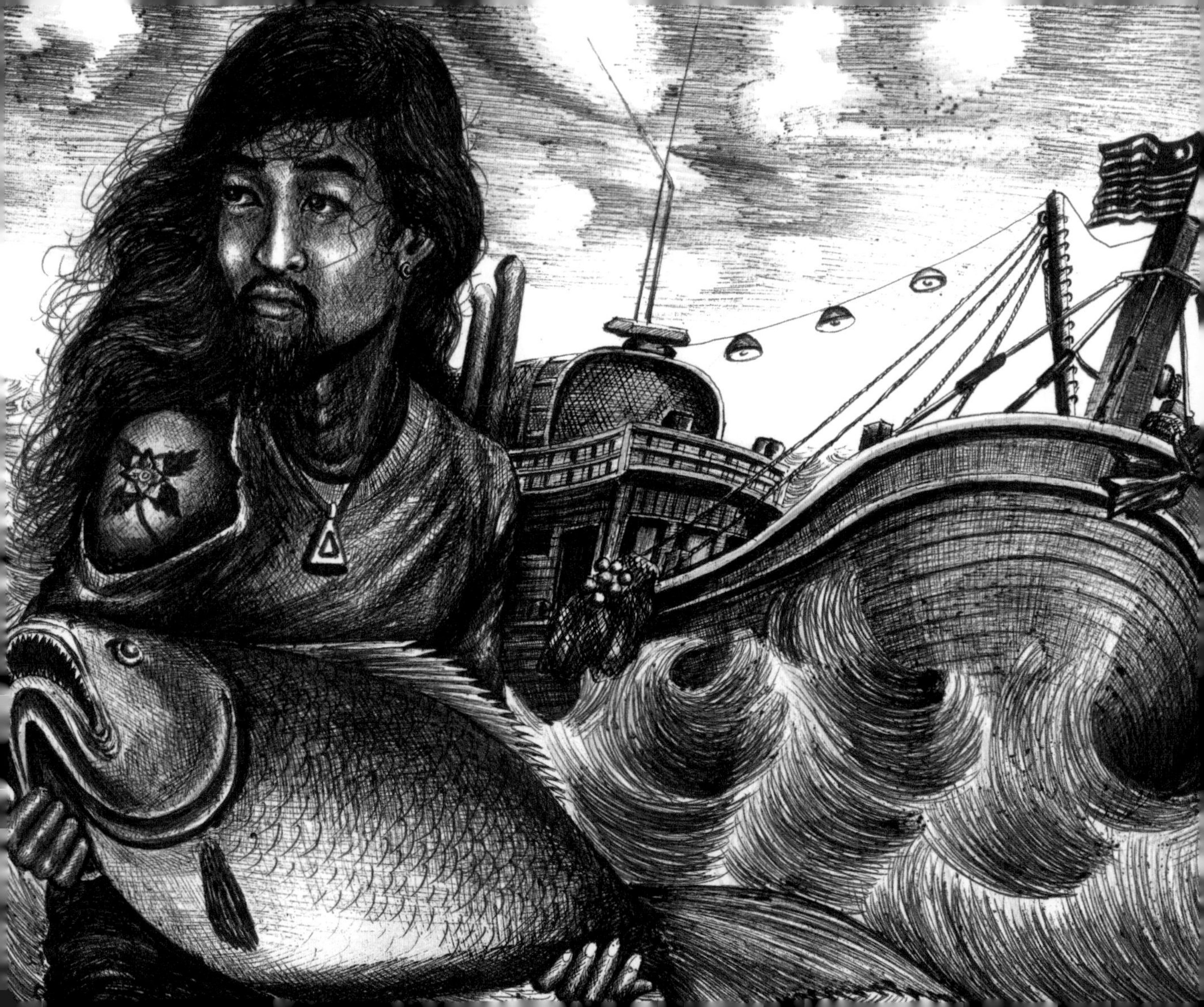

STORMS AT SEA

THE WEATHER WAS ALWAYS gray and rainy, like there were no seasons at all. Storms blew all the time. First it would start raining, and then the sky would turn black. In some storms, the waves were taller than palm trees. They'd bear down and we would hold our breath as the ship's engine climbed the face, and then the ship would fall over the lip with a sickening lurch. At sea the thunder was so loud you felt the shock inside your body. It made you sick, like an explosion.

WHEN THE STORMS WERE BAD EVERYONE PRAYED—THE CREW, THE *HOU NA,* THE CAPTAIN, everyone. I prayed to the Spirit of the Sea, the Lord of the Deep. I prayed to the God of Land and the God of Water. *"Let me live. Lord, don't let me die tonight."* The air was so full of water we could hardly breathe. Wet and terrified, we cowered, looking for something that'd keep us afloat if the next wave took us down.

MEN ON OTHER BOATS WERE SWEPT
away and never seen again. Clinging to my
floating prison, I knew that I could die at
any moment and just disappear beneath
the sea without a trace. No one would
ever care or know.

WHEN THE WIND SUBSIDED AND THE RAIN
stopped, everything was so quiet. The sky was clean.
The world had been washed. It was beautiful, and a
peace settled upon the ocean that had nothing at all to
do with our lives, adrift on a hellish ship and lost at sea.

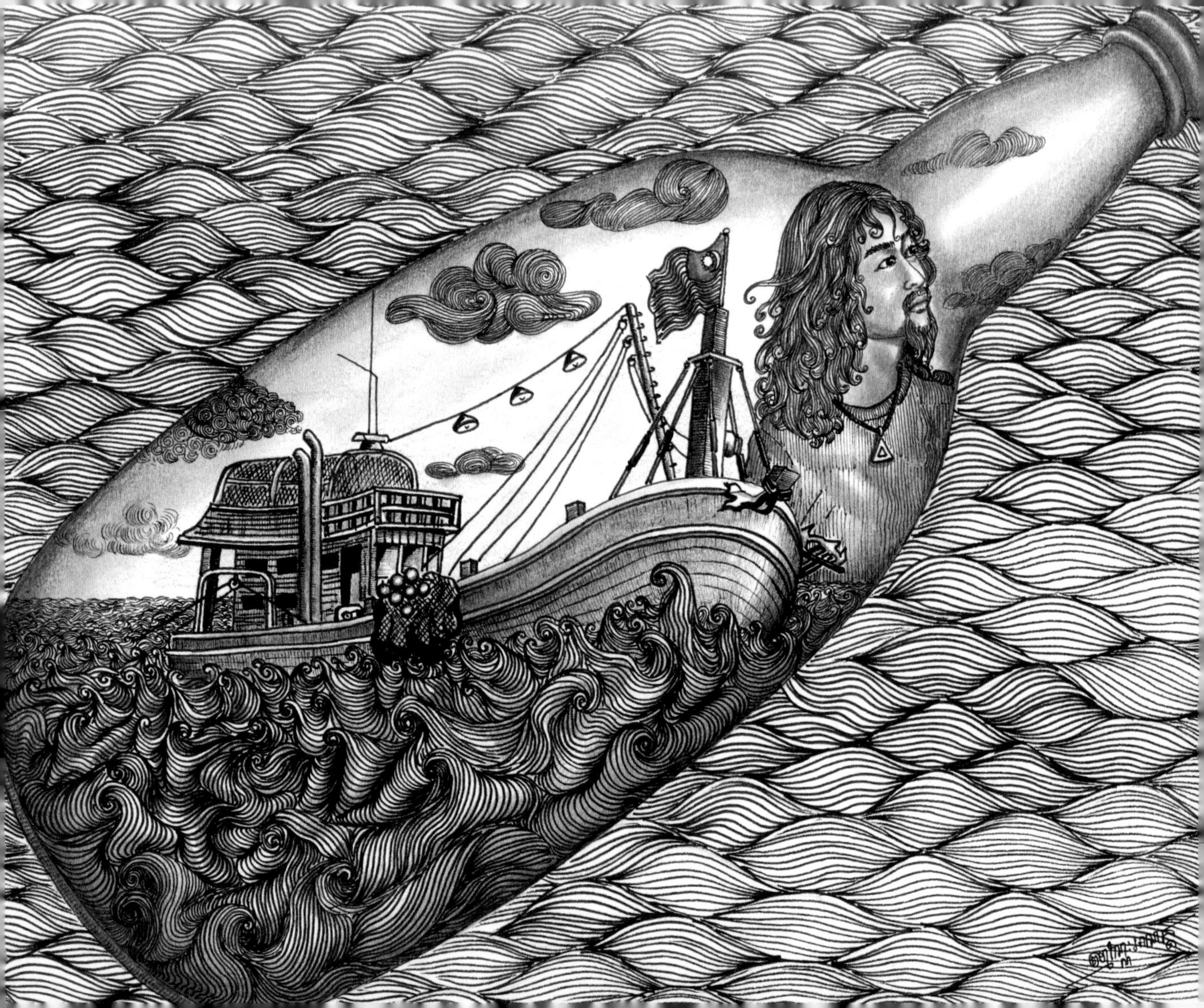

DAYS STRETCH OUT

ថ្ងៃឆ្ងាយទៅរាប់

THE DAYS WENT ROUND UNTIL THEY seemed endless. I was so bored. I no longer knew what day, month, or even year it was. The boat became the whole world. Life seemed so strange. Sometimes the sea teemed with dolphins. Sometimes whale plumes punctuated the horizon. Sometimes thousands of sharks surrounded us, staring up as they soared through the water on their fins.

ONE NIGHT I SAW A SWARM OF FIREFLIES FAR OUT
at sea. At first I thought it was a ghost coming to
me. It looked like fire suspended over the waves.
I watched for a long time, wondering if maybe
this was the spirit that watches over men at sea.

THE DEAD EYE AND THE DEEP BLUE SEA

THE NEXT DAY A LARGE WHITE
bird landed on the deck of the boat. It
seemed sick and was too weak to fly
away, but I couldn't see any wounds
or injuries. It was very thin and
obviously starving.

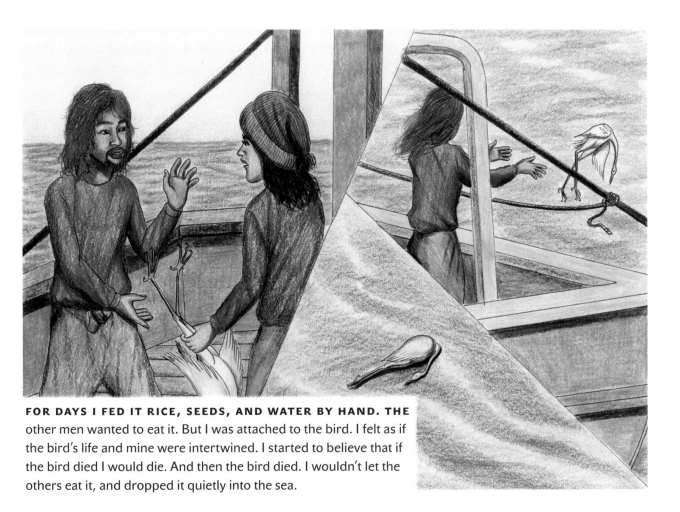

FOR DAYS I FED IT RICE, SEEDS, AND WATER BY HAND. THE other men wanted to eat it. But I was attached to the bird. I felt as if the bird's life and mine were intertwined. I started to believe that if the bird died I would die. And then the bird died. I wouldn't let the others eat it, and dropped it quietly into the sea.

ALL THE TIME, WHETHER WORKING OR RESTING, I WAS FILLED
with thoughts about my life and my place in this world. It must have been years
since I'd seen dry land. Why was the world so full of water? Why so many fish
and dead bodies? I was scared I would never escape. I'd be trapped forever.
I knew that one day I would have to jump into that endless ocean to be free.

"Do you know who I am and who you are? I do not want to be your slave anymore. One day I will stop you from trafficking people in this world!

—VANNAK ANAN PRUM

ESCAPE

ការគេចខ្លួន

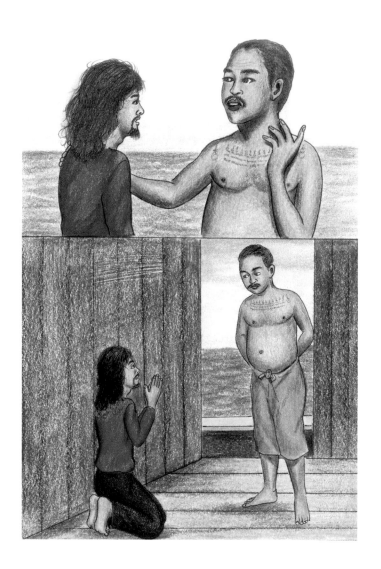

I NEVER STOPPED ASKING THE captain when I would leave. I asked every time the *took tho* arrived. He laughed and said, *"Soon, soon. Why are you in such a hurry? We'll get to shore soon!"* I would get down on my knees and beg.

HE WOULD SLAP ME: *"GET OUT OF my face!"* I stayed there. He got angry and yelled, *"You want another slap?"* I forced myself to control my reactions, and just looked down and walked away.

ONE DAY I OVERHEARD THE BOSS TALKING
on the radio about paying a fishing tax in Malaysia.
My heart sank. A new license meant we would be
at sea for years. But then he mentioned going to
Malaysia to get the license. This was to be my chance.

FOR MONTHS, I WORKED HARD TO MAKE THE CAPTAIN
like me. I listened to what he said and always complimented
him. I made myself extra useful, getting whatever he
needed and giving him massages every day. I kept my head
down, didn't talk much, and worked even harder.

ALL I THOUGHT ABOUT WAS ESCAPE. I FEARED ONLY TWO things: that I wouldn't escape, and that I would be trapped there forever. Months passed. I began to form a different plan in case we didn't go to Malaysia. I'd heard of crews that had mutinied. I planned to kidnap the captain and lock him in his quarters. Then we would force the boat to go to Malaysia.

THEN ONE DAY IN JUNE 2009 WE SAW land on the horizon. Everyone stopped and stared, all of us overwhelmed. I was so excited. But then a dinghy came to get the boss, and it was gone before I could try and get on board. Then I knew, I would have to jump overboard and swim to shore.

THE SWIM

ការប្រឡងទឹក

THE BOAT ANCHORED FAR FROM SHORE. WE DIDN'T REALLY KNOW WHERE WE WERE, NORTH or south. How far from Cambodia? How to even get there? But this was my only chance. In the middle of the night, I snuck out on deck with a Thai man called Chaya. Silently, we both emptied two fish sauce containers to use as our swimming floats.

WE TIED THE CONTAINERS TO OUR WRISTS and jumped into the water. No one heard our splash over the sound of the engine. For a while we hid in the boat's shadow to make sure no one had noticed. Then we swam for our lives to get clear of the boat's spotlights. I didn't look back, I just thought of my mother and prayed the whole way.

THE DEAD EYE AND THE DEEP BLUE SEA

IT TOOK A LONG TIME BUT FINALLY WE FELT THE BEACH BENEATH
our feet and staggered up the shore. We looked back out to sea. The boat's
lights were on, but there was no movement. They hadn't noticed we were
gone. I checked my camera, but it was ruined. Still, I didn't care. I was elated.
I'd made it. For the first time in more than three years, I was on land.

WE WERE STILL WORRIED WE MIGHT BE
missed, so we walked deep into the jungle. Then we
found a tall tree and climbed high up in its branches
to hide. There, up in the canopy, we fell into an
exhausted sleep. I was free.

THE MONKEYS AND THE MAN WAITING FOR US

ស្វា និង ឌ

IN THE MORNING WHEN WE WOKE, WE WERE NOT alone. Hundreds of yellow eyes were watching us: a troop of brown monkeys perched in the branches all around. They chased us to the ground, gnashing their teeth and screaming in our faces. We flicked branches in front of their eyes, and when they closed their eyes, we quietly backed away and ran back to the beach.

WE PAUSED AT THE EDGE OF THE trees and looked out to see if our ship was still there. It was gone. I was relieved, but I still thought they'd return when they realized we'd escaped.

THE DEAD EYE AND THE DEEP BLUE SEA

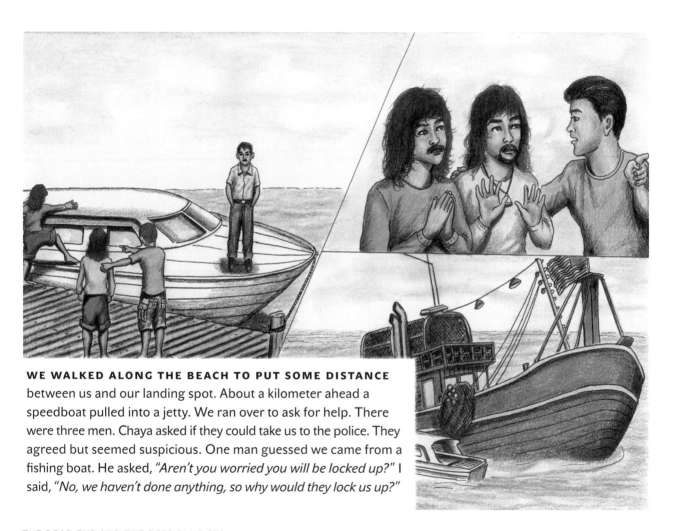

WE WALKED ALONG THE BEACH TO PUT SOME DISTANCE between us and our landing spot. About a kilometer ahead a speedboat pulled into a jetty. We ran over to ask for help. There were three men. Chaya asked if they could take us to the police. They agreed but seemed suspicious. One man guessed we came from a fishing boat. He asked, *"Aren't you worried you will be locked up?"* I said, *"No, we haven't done anything, so why would they lock us up?"*

WE GOT ON THE BOAT AND ALMOST IMMEDIATELY THE MEN BEGAN
insulting us. The driver said, *"You must have been too weak to be fishermen."* The
others said, *"No, I reckon they were just too lazy."* We sat on the edge of the boat
so we could jump off if they tried anything. When we arrived, another man was
already there waiting for us. It was strange. How did he know that we were coming?

THE DEAD EYE AND THE DEEP BLUE SEA

POLICE AND THE CHINESE MAN

ប៉ូលិស និងបុរសចិន

THE MAN ON THE SHORE KNEW THE
men on the boat. They told us he would
drive us to the police station. On the way,
he stopped to buy us some steamed rice.
We hadn't eaten since we'd escaped. We
drove for hours. It was night when we
arrived at the police station.

A POLICEMAN MET OUR CAR. HE ASKED US WHERE WE came from, but I didn't speak Malay. I gestured for a paper and pencil, then drew a picture of an airplane and Cambodia. In English I said, "*Go back, go back.*" The policemen shook their heads. They didn't understand. The first policeman made a phone call. A few minutes later, a non-uniformed man arrived. They went behind a glass door and I could see them talking about us. I was really worried. How could I make them understand?

WE WAITED AT THE STATION FOR ABOUT AN HOUR.
Then we were taken outside and put into a black car.
It wasn't a police car. The driver was Malaysian. He was
wearing a soccer jersey, not a police uniform. His wife was
in the car as well, sitting in the passenger seat. Neither of
them talked to us as the car pulled away from the station.

WE DROVE FOR TWO HOURS. I COULDN'T UNDERSTAND why they were taking us so far away. Was there a special jail in another province? Maybe immigration police were taking us into custody. Then, in the middle of nowhere, we pulled over and another car stopped alongside. Three Chinese men got out, all covered in tattoos. They told us to get into their car. As I stepped into the backseat I saw one Chinese man give the driver a stack of money. In a dead voice, Chaya said, *"We have been sold again."*

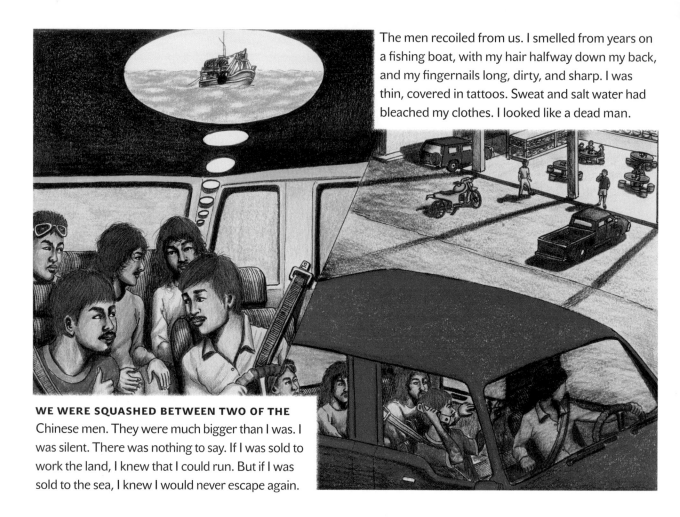

The men recoiled from us. I smelled from years on a fishing boat, with my hair halfway down my back, and my fingernails long, dirty, and sharp. I was thin, covered in tattoos. Sweat and salt water had bleached my clothes. I looked like a dead man.

WE WERE SQUASHED BETWEEN TWO OF THE Chinese men. They were much bigger than I was. I was silent. There was nothing to say. If I was sold to work the land, I knew that I could run. But if I was sold to the sea, I knew I would never escape again.

WE DROVE TO A RESTAURANT. THEY BOUGHT US two bowls of rice. Our captors had breakfast with another Chinese man. The men joked around like friends on a night out. Then they counted out the money it had cost to buy and sell us, right there on the table for everyone to see.

IT WAS CLEAR FROM HIS FACE THAT CHAYA HAD LOST ALL hope. He pushed his rice away. I said, *"Eat it. You'll need the strength to run. I don't want to go without you."* We left the restaurant as the sun was rising. Oil palm plantations lined the roads for miles and miles. Chaya fell asleep. I stayed awake so I could remember the way back.

CRAZY BOSS

NOT LONG AFTER SUNRISE WE
arrived at a plantation. The driver ordered
us out of the car while a strange-looking
man clambered down from the biggest
hut. He was carrying a huge gun, wearing
nothing but underwear and a neck scarf.
I soon learned that this was all he ever
wore. He looked crazy but acted friendly.
He looked me right in the eyes and
smiled, so I smiled back. He introduced
himself as *"Mr. Din,"* but I called him
"Crazy Boss."

* **"Do you know me? I'm the boss and my
name is Mr Din. My plantation is located in
Balingian village, Mukah division, Sarawak
in Malaysia."**

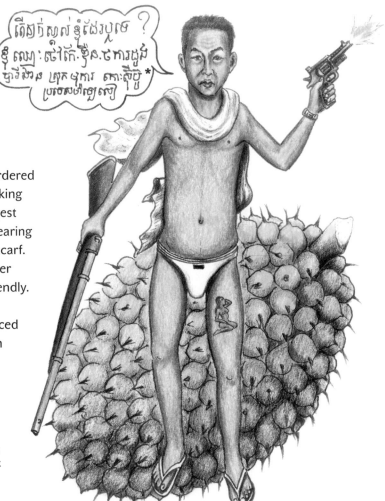

WE WERE SHOWN OUR SLEEPING QUARTERS, AND given work clothes, tools, a mat, a bed net, and a small stove on which we had to cook our own meals. Crazy Boss told us these were our possessions now, but we would have to work to pay him back for the cost.

THE DEAD EYE AND THE DEEP BLUE SEA

CRAZY BOSS SHOWED US THE CANTEEN WHERE ALL THE FOOD
was cooked. Because he could speak Thai, Chaya was able to
talk with him. He gave us rice, and while we ate he asked where
we had come from. When we finished breakfast, he asked if we
felt fit to work. I said yes because I needed him to like me.

WORK ON THIS PLANTATION WAS varied. We cut grass or collected the palm fruits that were used to make oil. Sometimes we dug holes. We started work at sunrise, and stopped when the sun went down. It was hard, tiring work, but a lot easier than life on the boat.

THE OTHER WORKERS CAME FROM MANY COUNTRIES—BURMA, MALAYSIA, THAILAND, THE PHILIPPINES. I MADE friends with a Timorese guy called Om. He had a passport. When he heard my story he said, *"I'm leaving in two months. I'll take you with me."* The farm supervisor rode around on a motorbike checking up on everyone. He asked us where we came from and wrote it down in his book. He patted me on the shoulder and said, *"Brother, you're a hard worker!"* He was unarmed, and I never saw him beat anyone. It really wasn't like the boat.

TO SUPPLEMENT OUR MEALS OF PLAIN rice, and to build up my strength, I made a hook out of wire and caught fish in a stream. After so much death on the boat, I didn't want to kill more fish, but I needed the energy. It was ironic that, even after escaping the boat, I was still fishing.

THE DEAD EYE AND THE DEEP BLUE SEA

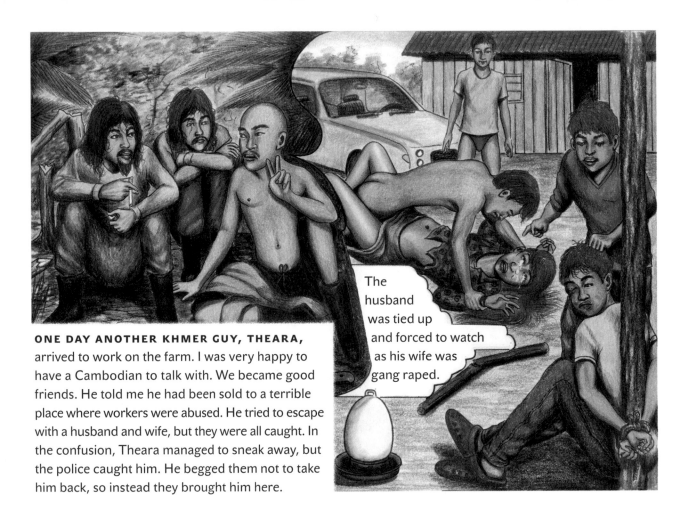

ONE DAY ANOTHER KHMER GUY, THEARA, arrived to work on the farm. I was very happy to have a Cambodian to talk with. We became good friends. He told me he had been sold to a terrible place where workers were abused. He tried to escape with a husband and wife, but they were all caught. In the confusion, Theara managed to sneak away, but the police caught him. He begged them not to take him back, so instead they brought him here.

The husband was tied up and forced to watch as his wife was gang raped.

THE PHONE

อรพิม
บ

DAYS QUICKLY PASSED, THEN weeks, and months. Everyone except those of us from Thailand, Burma, and Cambodia could come and go as they wished. Escape was always on my mind. I knew I would need money and a passport. Crazy Boss said, *"If you work hard, I'll send you home one day."* I no longer worried about beatings, sinking, or storms. But I was still a prisoner there, a slave, never paid for my labor.

CRAZY BOSS ALWAYS CARRIED A GUN. ONCE I was walking past his cabin as he was shooting a big new rifle. I asked, *"Can I try?"* He smiled his crazy smile and handed me the weapon. I pointed it straight at him. He shouted, *"Hey, what are you doing, shoot that way!"* I smiled, too, and said, *"I just wanted to know if it was a powerful gun."* I pointed the gun away from him and pulled the trigger.

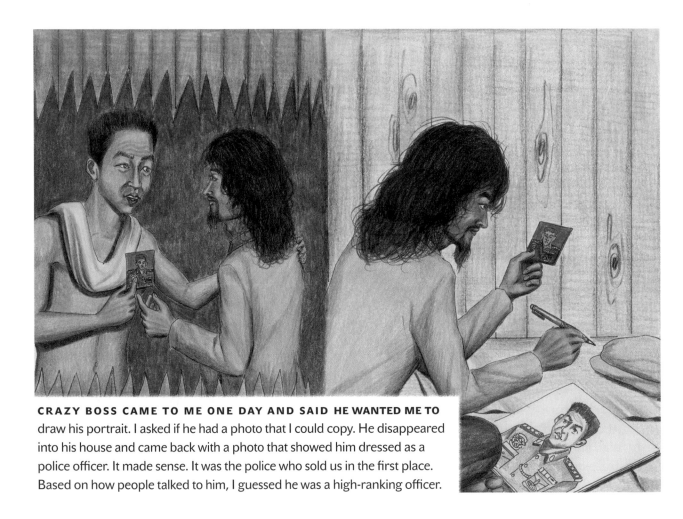

CRAZY BOSS CAME TO ME ONE DAY AND SAID HE WANTED ME TO
draw his portrait. I asked if he had a photo that I could copy. He disappeared
into his house and came back with a photo that showed him dressed as a
police officer. It made sense. It was the police who sold us in the first place.
Based on how people talked to him, I guessed he was a high-ranking officer.

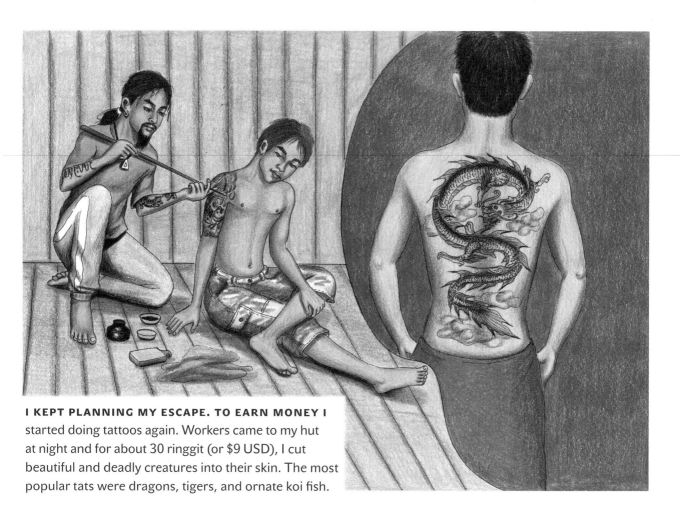

I KEPT PLANNING MY ESCAPE. TO EARN MONEY I started doing tattoos again. Workers came to my hut at night and for about 30 ringgit (or $9 USD), I cut beautiful and deadly creatures into their skin. The most popular tats were dragons, tigers, and ornate koi fish.

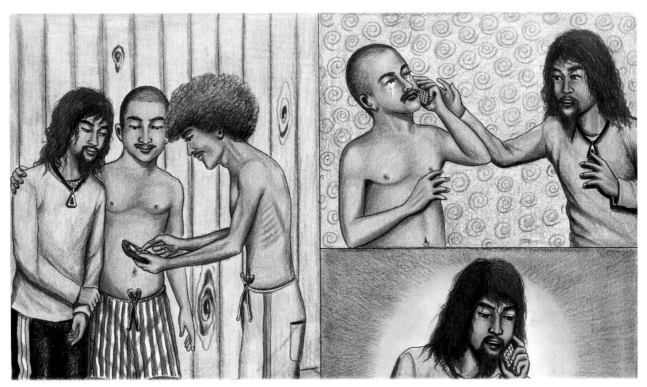

EVENTUALLY I SAVED ENOUGH TO BUY A MOBILE PHONE. OM GOT IT FOR ME. HOLDING IT, FOR the first time in five years I was linked to the "real world." Theara remembered his mother's phone number. We dialed it. It rang, and she answered. Theara was overcome, crying, and making no sense. We didn't have much credit, so I grabbed the phone and told her what had happened. She asked, *"Where are you?"* Om said, *"Balingian, near Mukah Commune, Sibu, Sarawak Island."* She promised to find help and begged us to be safe. Then our credit ran out and the line was cut.

THAT AFTERNOON WE WENT ABOUT OUR work as if it was just a normal day. But I felt more alive than ever before. I was filled with a new hope that I might get to see my home again. To make sure we didn't raise any suspicions, I worked harder than ever.

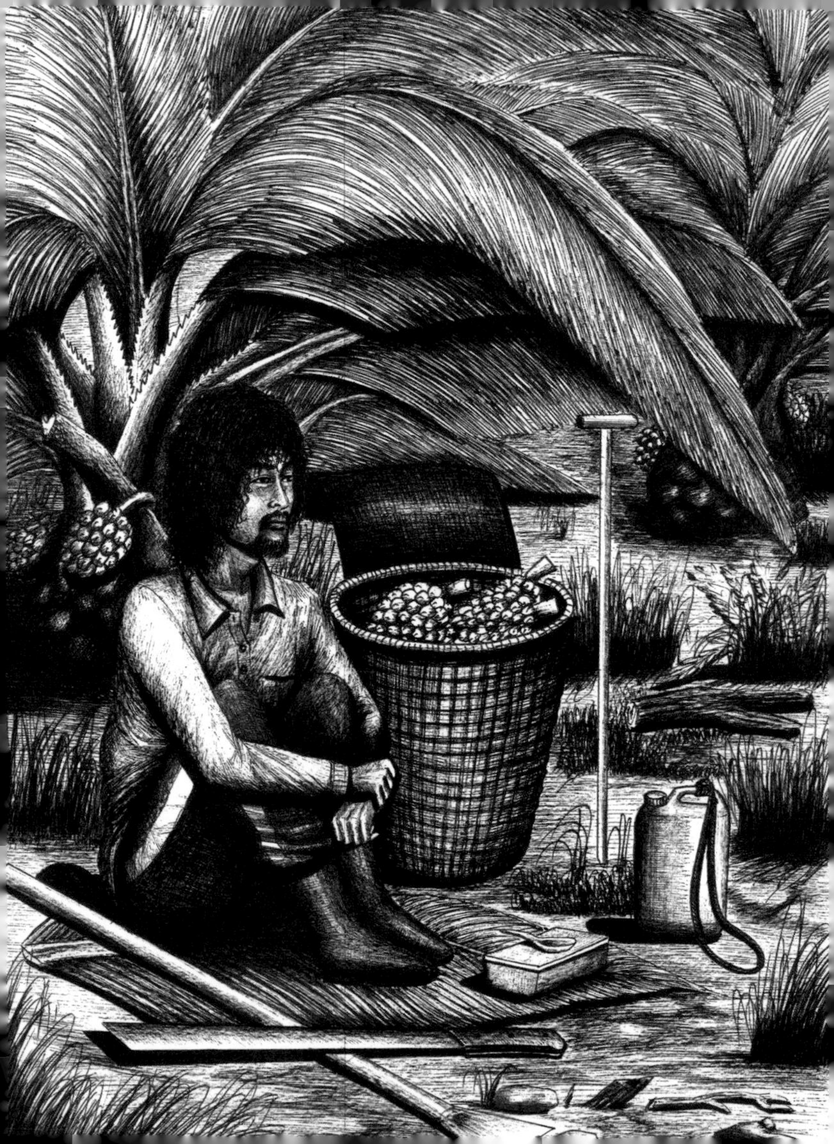

THE FIGHT

ការប្រយុទ្ធពាគ្គ៌ វាយតប

THAT NIGHT OM FELT like throwing a party and bought some wine and beer in town. Everyone got pretty well drunk. A Burmese guy started bickering with a Thai man over a cigarette lighter. Angry words turned into a shoving match. More guys got involved, Thai versus Burmese. Suddenly, someone had a knife. And then everyone had a blade. Just like that, without warning, we were in danger.

THEARA STEPPED INTO THE MIDDLE TO TRY AND REASON WITH THEM: *"BROTHERS, WE'RE ALL in the same mess. Please don't fight each other."* No one listened. Instead, a Burmese guy raised his machete and hit Theara on the back of the head several times. Theara fell to the ground, with blood pouring out of a deep wound. I jumped in and held Theara, yelling, *"Stop it, stop!"* Someone hit me in the neck with a machete before Om and a couple of other guys separated the group, and the fighting died down.

THEARA WAS COVERED IN BLOOD, BARELY
conscious, and moaning. I carried him to the field
manager and said, *"Look at his head. Please, he
needs a hospital."* They put us in the back of a truck.
I was bleeding from my neck. I thought about my wife
and child, trying to imagine their faces. I wanted to see
them. We had come so close to freedom.

ON THE WAY, THE DRIVER GOT WORRIED about being caught with two badly wounded slaves. He waved down a police car and told them he just found us like this, and that he didn't know us or where we were from. They put us in their car and took us to a hospital. We were lucky these were not the policemen who had sold us.

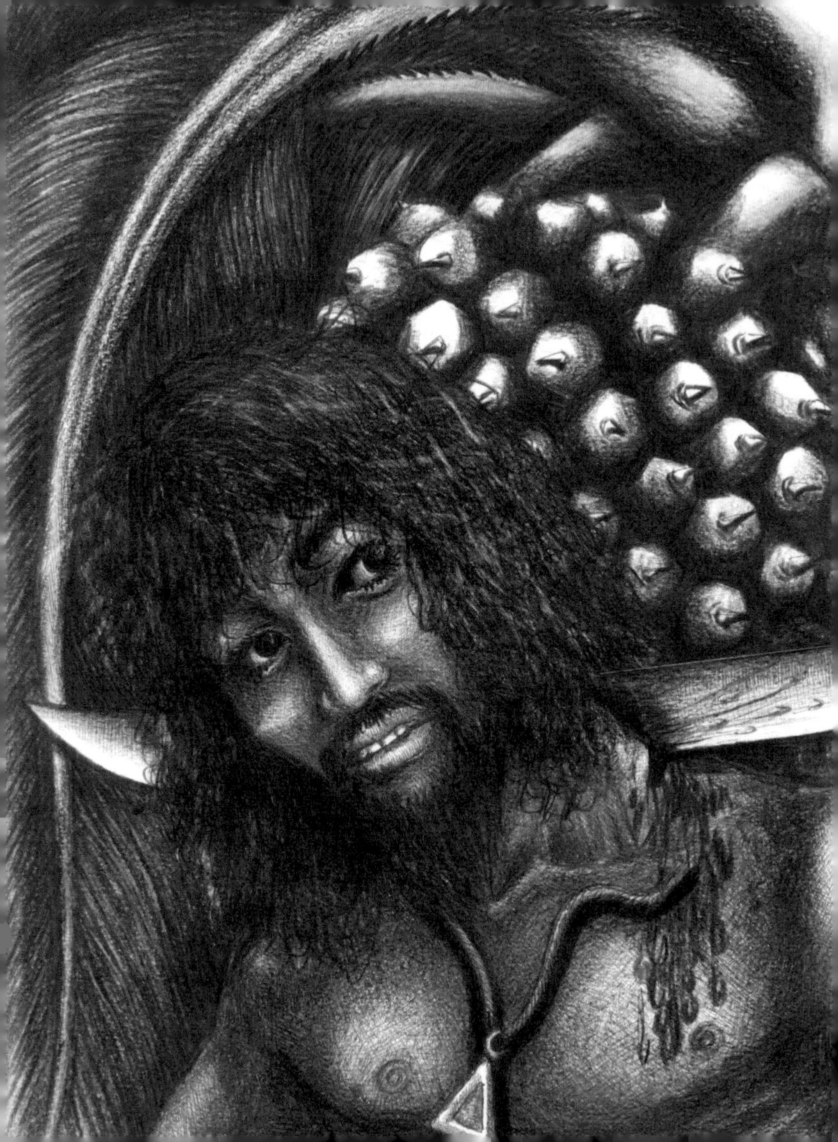

HOSPITAL

อูรธิต
ป

AT THE HOSPITAL THEARA COULDN'T walk and was incoherent with pain. I was wet with blood and also in a lot of pain, but my wound wasn't deep. I was more worried about Theara. The wound on his head was gaping, and he was lapsing in and out of consciousness. Even if he survived, would he ever get his mind back? Would he be able to speak again? While the doctors treated him, I stayed close to make sure we weren't separated.

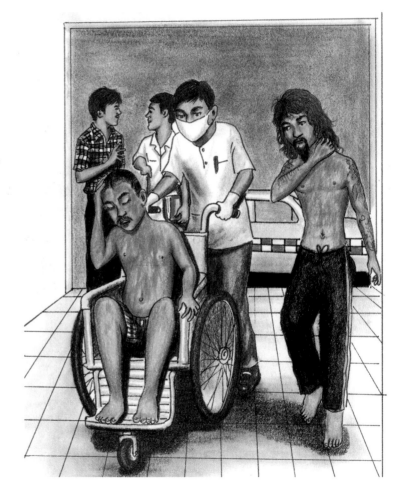

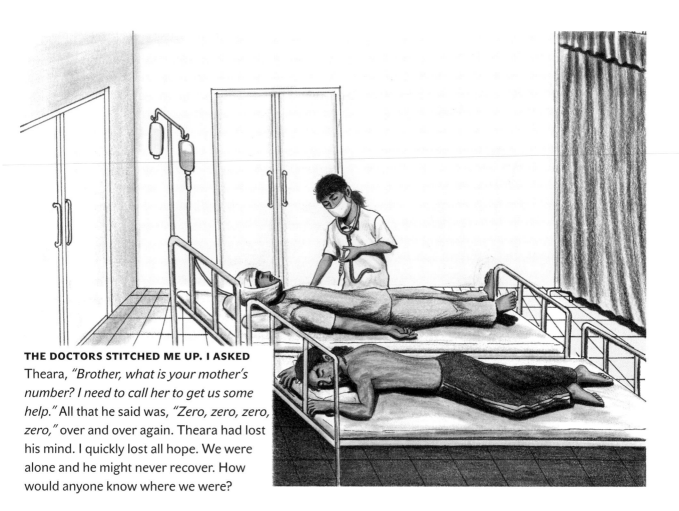

THE DOCTORS STITCHED ME UP. I ASKED Theara, *"Brother, what is your mother's number? I need to call her to get us some help."* All that he said was, *"Zero, zero, zero, zero,"* over and over again. Theara had lost his mind. I quickly lost all hope. We were alone and he might never recover. How would anyone know where we were?

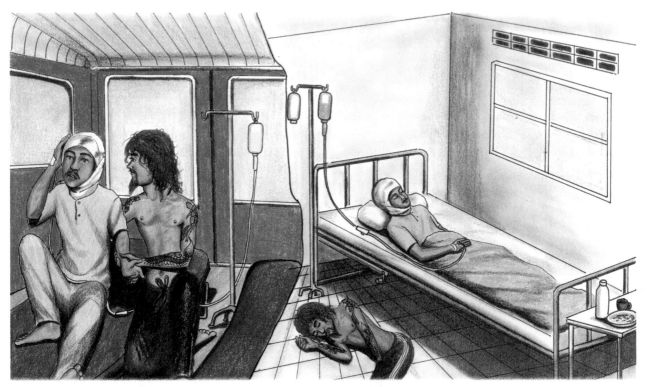

THE DOCTORS SAID THEARA HAD TO GO TO A LARGER HOSPITAL. I BEGGED TO GO ALONG WITH
him. I said I was the only one who spoke Khmer, so they let me go. On the way, Theara writhed and screamed in pain. When we arrived the nurses put Theara in a bed, and gave him plenty of food and medicine. I slept on the floor next to him in my blood-soaked clothes. I received no medicine or food. I kept asking Theara for his mother's number. All he would say was, *"Zero, zero, zero, zero."*

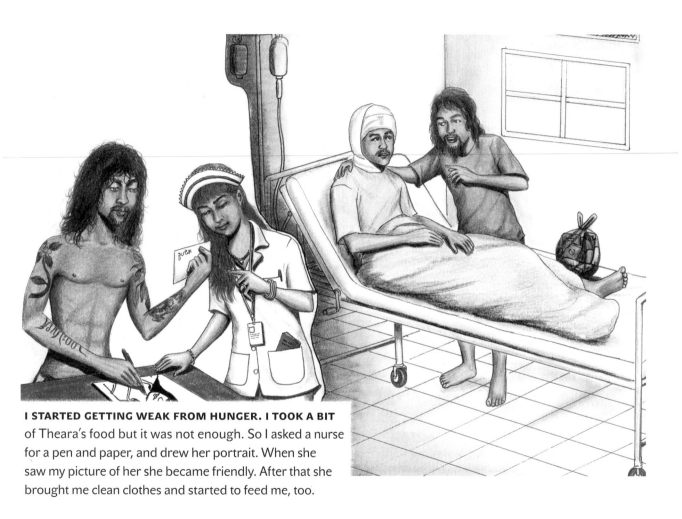

I STARTED GETTING WEAK FROM HUNGER. I TOOK A BIT of Theara's food but it was not enough. So I asked a nurse for a pen and paper, and drew her portrait. When she saw my picture of her she became friendly. After that she brought me clean clothes and started to feed me, too.

OVER THE NEXT FEW DAYS THEARA CAME BACK TO LIFE. HE REMEMBERED HIS mother's number and I called her on the hospital phone. She asked what had happened. I told her we were being kept at Sibu Hospital, Sarawak. She contacted an organization called LICADHO, and three days later an official from the Cambodian embassy visited us. He promised they would soon get us home. But we waited for two weeks, and then we were sent to jail.

IN JAIL THE GUARDS GAVE US PRISON
uniforms and locked us in a tiny cell. We were told
nothing. Theara's wounds were almost healed. His
head had been shaved. The cell was so small that
we couldn't walk around, and we spent all day just
sitting down.

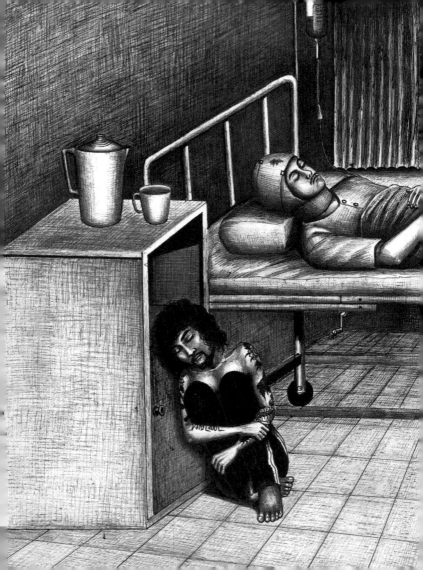

YO-YO JUSTICE

ພຸ ກຸ ທ ຫ ຕ ລ ນ ກ ເ ຮ

WE WAITED IN that cramped cell, not knowing why we were being held, or how long we would be there. I was overwhelmed by depression. Theara and I talked only about our families and going home. We never left the cell, and all our questions were met with silence. We tried not to forget that Theara's mother was out there working to help us.

AFTER TEN DAYS, A TALL GERMAN MAN CALLED MANFRED
Hornung and a Khmer man named Prak Socheat came to visit us. They
sat with us for a long time, listening and writing down everything we
said. Manfred was kind. He said, *"I cannot say when, but I promise you
will get out. I need to follow Malaysian laws, but sooner or later you
will go home."*

THE DEAD EYE AND THE DEEP BLUE SEA

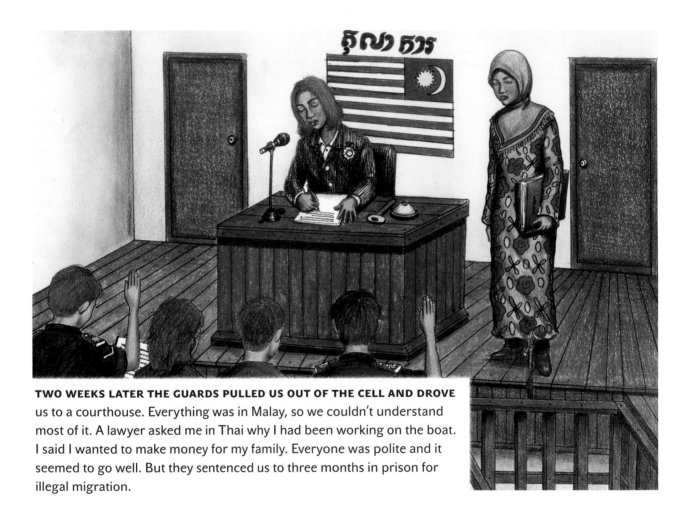

TWO WEEKS LATER THE GUARDS PULLED US OUT OF THE CELL AND DROVE
us to a courthouse. Everything was in Malay, so we couldn't understand
most of it. A lawyer asked me in Thai why I had been working on the boat.
I said I wanted to make money for my family. Everyone was polite and it
seemed to go well. But they sentenced us to three months in prison for
illegal migration.

WE WERE TAKEN TO A PRISON IN MUKAH. THEARA was still recovering from his injuries and slept the whole way. I couldn't sleep. I couldn't stop thinking about my family, my wife and child. How old would my daughter be by now, nearly five? I couldn't stop worrying. What would happen to us now?

THE DEAD EYE AND THE DEEP BLUE SEA

WE WERE ONLY AT MUKAH PRISON FOR A FEW DAYS WHEN I WAS TAKEN TO A police station. There the policeman led me to a window looking in on another room, where two men were talking and laughing. One was the station's commander. With a shock I recognized the other man instantly. It was Crazy Boss. Suddenly I understood the fictional court case, and prison sentences. I remembered the photo. Crazy Boss was at least a provincial or a district police chief.

THE POLICEMAN ASKED, *"HAVE YOU SEEN THIS MAN BEFORE?"* I said yes. He asked, *"Did he enslave you?"* I looked at him. I knew right then he wanted me to lie. He asked, *"Do you want to stay in jail for the next twenty-five years?"* I said no. He asked me again, *"Do you know this man, and did he enslave you?"* I said no. He seemed satisfied. They took me back to jail.

WEEKS PASSED. THEN WE WERE TRANSFERRED by plane to a prison in Kuala Lumpur. This prison was filled with people from all over the world, many different nationalities. They kept moving Theara and me around. It seemed as if they didn't know what to do with us.

A FEW WEEKS LATER WE WERE SENT BACK TO MUKAH PRISON AND TAKEN STRAIGHT TO THE POLICE STATION. A different policeman interrogated us, hitting the table to scare us. He said, *"What's going to happen to your family if you're in jail for the next twenty years? What are your children going to eat? Do you ever want to see them again?"* I missed my family so much that I almost couldn't bear it anymore. Who would I become after twenty years in prison? I agreed to lie. The policeman tapped the table: knock, knock, *"That's good, Vannak. Very good."*

THE DEAD EYE AND THE DEEP BLUE SEA

CRAZY BOSS WAS WAITING FOR US OUTSIDE THE STATION.
He said hello and acted as if we were friends. I looked him
in the eye and asked for money. He smiled and gave me 100
ringgit (about $28 USD), and some fruit. Then he invited me
to come back and visit anytime I wanted. I quietly took the
money and fruit.

THE DEAD EYE AND THE DEEP BLUE SEA

THE POLICE HOUSED US IN A MEETING ROOM IN the station for about a month. They gave us food and clothes. The station commander told us we would be released very soon, and we were free to walk around the station. Everyone was friendly and I ended up drawing pictures for almost all of them. When we left, they wished us good luck and asked us to visit again if we should ever return.

BUT WE WERE NOT YET FREE. INSTEAD WE were transferred to a larger prison in Sibu. It was a very scary place, surrounded by soldiers and high walls. Looking up I could see just a tiny piece of sky. It felt like living at the bottom of a well.

THEY SHAVED OUR HEADS ANDLOCKED us up in a cell with twenty other men. The people imprisoned there came from all over the world.

THERE WAS ONE MEAL EVERY DAY: WHITE RICE WITH BEAN CAKE, OR plain fish. The guards were constantly doing spot checks. Anyone who didn't have a passport was beaten with a rubber hose. Theara and I never knew what might happen next, so we stuck together at all times to make sure we weren't separated. Luckily we were only there for a few days, so they never got around to beating us.

NEXT THEY TRANSFERRED US TO A jail in the mountains. We were moved so often we started joking that we were on a tour of Malaysia's best prisons. In prison you had to pay for everything except one basic meal, so prisoners paid for extra food, for clothing, and for cigarettes. People without money went hungry and had to beg. But Theara and I didn't need money. Crazy Boss paid for everything. We just had to say his name.

PRISON

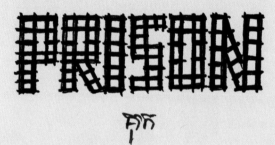

OUR ORIGINAL sentence was three months, but in the end it was seven months and one day before we were told we'd be going home. They sent us to a place called the Lenggeng Jail. This was where prisoners were processed for release. We waited two more weeks before the Cambodian embassy came to collect us.

THE DEAD EYE AND THE DEEP BLUE SEA

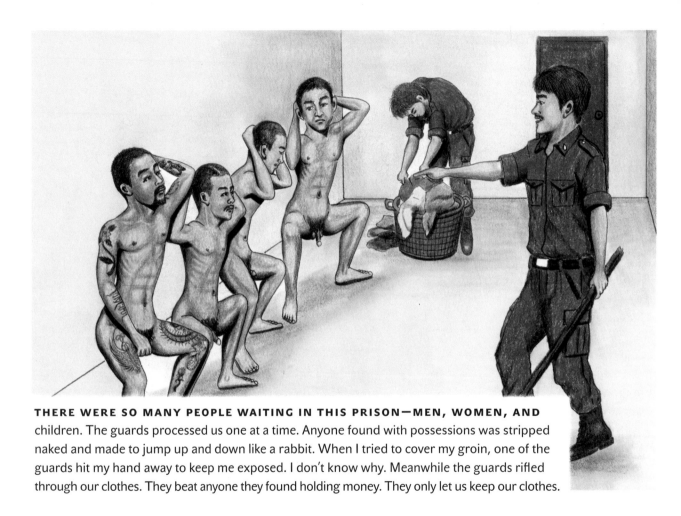

THERE WERE SO MANY PEOPLE WAITING IN THIS PRISON—MEN, WOMEN, AND
children. The guards processed us one at a time. Anyone found with possessions was stripped
naked and made to jump up and down like a rabbit. When I tried to cover my groin, one of the
guards hit my hand away to keep me exposed. I don't know why. Meanwhile the guards rifled
through our clothes. They beat anyone they found holding money. They only let us keep our clothes.

A FEW DAYS LATER A KHMER WOMAN VISITED US. SHE WAS DRESSED LIKE A MALAYSIAN and said, *"If you give me 900,000 riel (or around $225 USD), I will fly you to your family right now, no delay."* I said, *"My family is poor, and we don't have that kind of money. But don't worry, sister. I don't need your help. I've got someone else who will help save me."* Some of the other prisoners did give her money, though. And they were sent home straight away.

FINALLY WE GOT THE GOOD NEWS FROM OUR EMBASSY. IN FIVE DAYS WE WERE TO BE FLOWN home. They now moved us to an immigration facility. It was full of Cambodians. I met a girl who worked as a maid for a rich family. She told me that the wife used to beat her all the time. Once the wife made her stand on one foot for an entire day because she was caught reading a book. She had no one helping her. I gave her everything I had. She gave me her family's address and begged me not to forget her. I promised, but somehow I lost her address on the way home.

THE DEAD EYE AND THE DEEP BLUE SEA

HOME

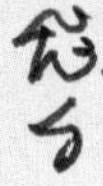

THE NEXT DAY, MAY 15, 2010 AT 8:00 A.M., after three years and seven months on a boat, four months on the plantation, one month in the hospital, and eight months in Malaysian police stations and jails, I boarded a plane bound for Cambodia.

THE PLANE TOOK OFF. I WATCHED THE GROUND FALL AWAY AND DIDN'T TAKE MY EYES AWAY FROM THE window until we landed. I watched the world slide past far beneath us. We flew over palm plantations and out over the sea. It stretched forever, the blue ocean far below, and me in the clouds. Then rice fields, lakes, and rivers. I was overwhelmed with excitement and nervousness, and filled with thoughts of my wife. I was close. I knew that I would see my home again.

THE DEAD EYE AND THE DEEP BLUE SEA

WHEN WE LANDED, MANFRED AND A GROUP
of LICADHO staff met us at the airport. I remember
their names: Komret, Chanta, Chea, Dara, and many
others. Everyone was so happy and friendly. They
all shook my hand and patted my back. "*Welcome
home!*" they said. It felt like a celebration.

WE DROVE TO LICADHO'S OFFICES, WHERE THEY HAD ARRANGED
for a monk to bless us. The monk prayed for us to be free of anger
and hatred. Everyone was chanting and blessing, but I didn't feel
angry. It felt incredible. I was just happy to be alive. I was gripped by
the strong need to draw. I asked Manfred for a pencil and some paper.

THE DEAD EYE AND THE DEEP BLUE SEA

AFTER THE BLESSING, MANFRED TOOK ME to Phnom Penh, where they had booked a room for me at the Thmey Guesthouse. He gave me food and new clothes. When he left I took my pencil out. In that quiet room I drew a picture of the fishing boat and me. When it was done I wrote on it, *"Today is a new day. Don't let the sun go down."*

THE NEXT MORNING MANFRED TOOK ME TO THE BUS STATION AND GAVE ME A TICKET HOME.
as the bus was starting to board, I gave my drawing to Manfred. When he saw what it was, he was shocked.
He held it close to his face to look at the details of the boat, and of me and the other men working. Then he
looked at me and said, *"Amazing, Vannak, amazing."*

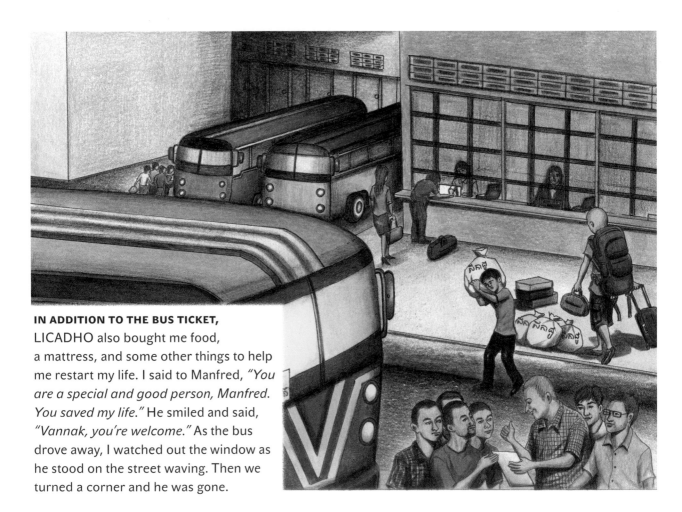

IN ADDITION TO THE BUS TICKET, LICADHO also bought me food, a mattress, and some other things to help me restart my life. I said to Manfred, *"You are a special and good person, Manfred. You saved my life."* He smiled and said, *"Vannak, you're welcome."* As the bus drove away, I watched out the window as he stood on the street waving. Then we turned a corner and he was gone.

THE BUS DROVE THROUGH THE busy streets of Phnom Penh. With the noise of traffic and horns in my ears, I closed my eyes and went to sleep.

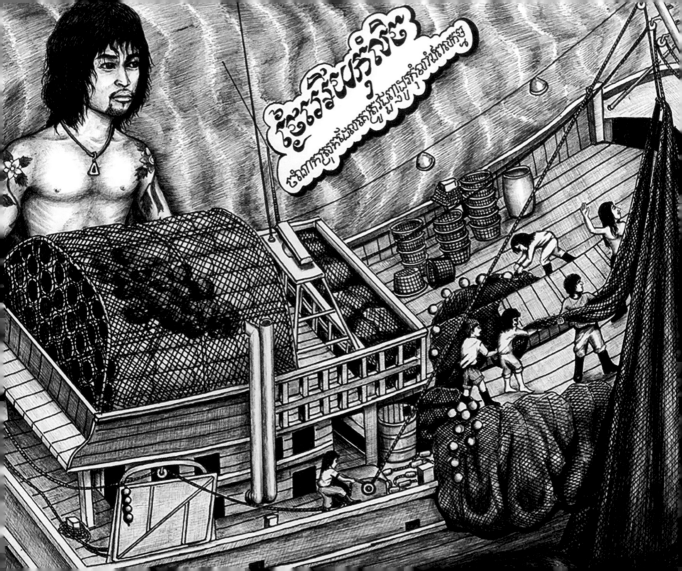

* Top line: "Today is a new day. Don't let the
Second line: "Workers who go abroad but
See page 216.

EPILOGUE

ចុងបញ្ចប់

I WOKE UP WHEN THE BUS STOPPED. I got out and stood on the main street of my old village. Everything had changed. There were factories now where before there had been rice fields. Everyone was talking on mobile phones. But as I walked down my street I could see that my house was the same as I left it, a small hut on a dusty road.

I SAW MY WIFE, SOKUN, WORKING IN the yard with a young girl playing at her feet. It was my daughter! But she was afraid of me. I was suddenly aware of how I must look. Sokun was angry and suspicious. I tried to explain— the moto and the middleman, the boat, the plantation, Crazy Boss, prisons—but she didn't believe me. I asked if I could stay, but she made me sleep outside. I spent the first night sitting in the dark, watching their faces as they slept. The next morning I left them to stay with a friend.

A FEW DAYS LATER MY WIFE CALLED ME.
Manfred had phoned to ask if I would draw my story.
As I drew my story, my wife and daughter looked on.
They got curious and came closer. When I finished,
my wife said to me, *"I thought you were lying. But now
I see it's the truth."* And so I drew my way back into my
family home.

NOW MY WIFE AND I HAVE A NEW BABY. BUT
there is still no work here. Making a living is no easier than
it was when I went to Thailand. I hear about others making
that same journey all the time. I wish I could make a living
drawing pictures. I want most of all to share my story. I've
met incredible people from all over the world who want to
hear my story. But I'm happiest when I'm at home.

Anytime, while I'm working or resting, walking or
sleeping, the memories can flood back in. My physical
injuries hurt less, but my memory is a wound that will
never heal. I struggle with the anger I feel toward the
people who sold me like an animal. I try to focus
on the Buddha, and to let go of hate. I don't want
to let this hellish experience destroy my life.

I want to stay in Cambodia. I don't want to live
anywhere else. For me, my homeland is priceless. It is
everything.

I love my life and my family. I love Cambodia, and I
love this world.

This is my true story.

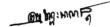

Vannak Anan Prum

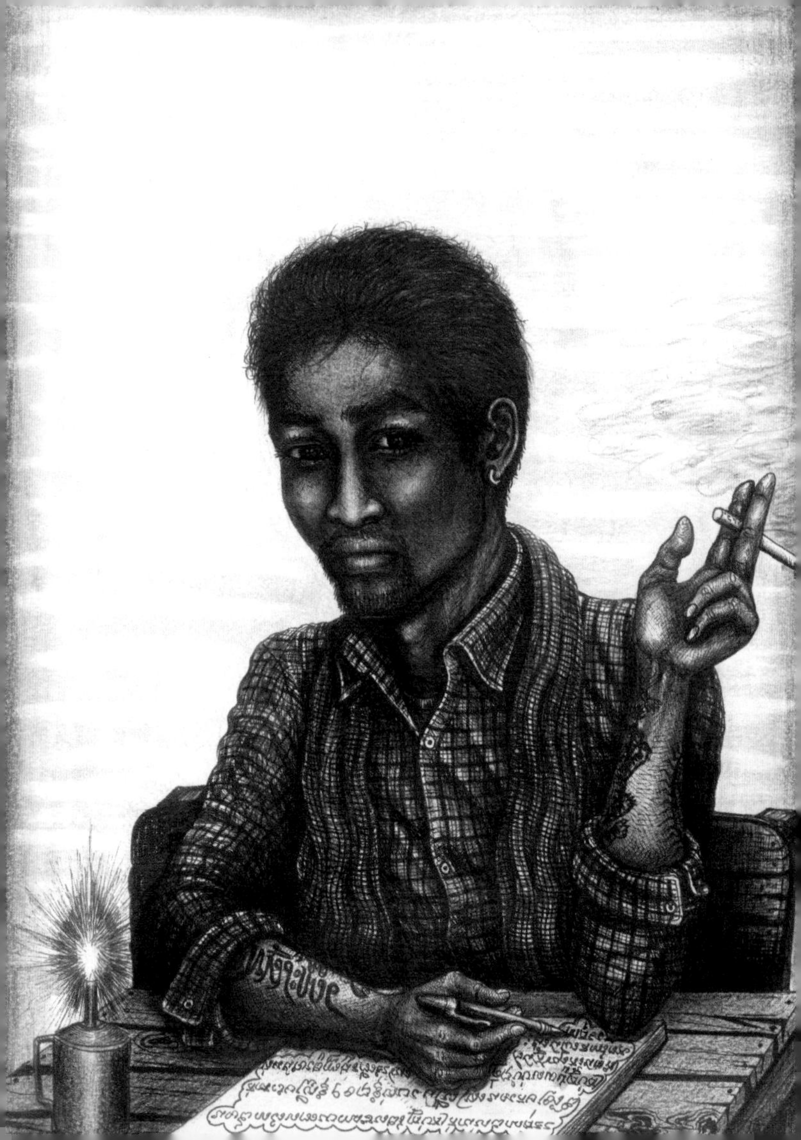

VANNAK ANAN PRUM is a Cambodian survivor of human trafficking. While looking for work on the Thai — Cambodian border, he was detained as a slave on a fishing boat, enduring hard labor and hellish treatment for four grueling years. After making his escape by literally jumping ship, Vannack was sold by his ostensible rescuers on the Malaysian coast to a plantation owner and police official. After another year of hard labor and imprisonment, a human rights organization helped him finally return to his family.

At home in Cambodia, he drew pictures of what he remembered to explain his whereabouts during the course of his years as a modern-day slave. Though never formally educated or trained in art, Vannak has loved drawing since childhood — from figures traced in the dirt, to tattos etched into skin, to these pencil and ink illustrations detailing his personal odyssey.

In 2012 US Secretary of State Hillary Clinton awarded Vannak the Human Rights Defender Award.

This is his story.

To support Vannak and see more of his artwork, visit his online store, https://.zazzle.com/vannakprum/.

AFTERWORD

THE VOICES of the enslaved are muted in the so-called "free world," where the practice of slavery can seem distant and archaic, almost unreal. Even when the practice is acknowledged as contemporary and all-too-close to home, those voices are frequently drowned out: as well-meaning supporters often attempt to speak for the enslaved, their "free world" prejudices oversimplify complex life stories, and the many factors contributing to a thriving global slave trade are reduced to the misdeeds of a few obvious villains.

When powerful and eloquent voices arise, like those of Frederick Douglass and Harriet Tubman in the past, or Minh Dang and Shamere McKenzie today, we are forced to reassess our simplistic notions of slavery's victims.

Though Douglass and Tubman were lionized in their time, they were also sidelined as symbols, and even today pat narrative histories overlook the true range of their intellect and activism. In this, the fourth great antislavery movement in human history, the critical question remains whether we will reject past assumptions and give our full attention to the profound knowledge of slavery that is held only by those who have lived through it.

In slavery all slaves are silenced, while in freedom two forces work to mute ex-slaves. The first is the economic and cultural system supporting slavery. Globally, most slaves live where enslavement receives at least partial support from powerful elites. Systems of oppression and discrimination, patriarchy, religious prejudice, and bias according to caste, class, or race are the foundations on which slavery is constructed. To end slavery it is necessary to change the systems that allow slavery to exist. Freed slaves, like Vannak Anan Prum, understand these systems of oppression perfectly, and see clearly how they operate. But these systems of hierarchy and oppression serve the powerful well, and speaking against them carries serious risks. In the countries where slavery is most prevalent today, the rich and their government agents prefer to have freed slaves remain silent, or simply disappear. Yet this suppression is less effective than the second, interior, force that mutes ex-slaves: the sense of shame and dislocation that wells up from within the former slave's own being.

The enslaved experience psychological damage similar to people subjected to sexual violence. Like victims of rape, ex-slaves often feel shame. This shame is irrational; the victims have not done anything wrong, indeed they have been very seriously wronged. But the stigma of enslavement, a product of long-term physical and psychological abuse by slaveholders, presses upon the minds and emotions of slaves long after they've gained their freedom, with enduring trauma to both their sense of self and self-expression. Is it any wonder that ex-slaves speaking for themselves may seem at times less than articulate, once we know of the pain that they carry? Overcoming shame can be a long process, but the very act of speaking and writing can be restorative. As Toni Morrison put it, "Freeing yourself was one thing; claiming ownership of that freed self was another."* That fact adds a special dimension to this book. The voice and drawings of Vannak Anan Prum both bring us the truth of slavery and illuminate a way to resolve and vanquish the pain of slavery for freed slaves.

Vannak Anan Prum was a child in rural Cambodia as that country was torn apart by the Khmer Rouge's genocidal campaign and the Vietnamese invasion which followed. Not surprisingly he grew up hungry and unschooled. Abused by his stepfather, he became a child soldier (a common form of child slavery around

---

* *Beloved* (New York: Alfred A. Knopf, 1987), p. 95.

the world even now), then a monk, and, after reaching adulthood, set out on his own. His existence was hand-to-mouth and only softened when he met and married his wife, Sokun. When she became pregnant with their first child, Vannak set off to find better work and earn money to support his family. At that moment he stepped onto the path that would lead him into slavery.

For slaveholders and human traffickers, outright kidnapping is generally a last resort, as there is little point in using force when they can play on the legitimate desires we all hold for a better life, funds and food for our families, and a chance to give our children a brighter future. Once Vannak crossed the border into Thailand in search of this better life, he was already entangled in the global system of human trafficking that in his case led to the fishing boats where many thousands are enslaved. These boats stay at sea for years, fishing illegally and overfishing in protected waters. Their captains use and abuse their enslaved workers, and often dispose of any who are too ill or injured to work.

Vannak's remarkable story and deeply moving drawings show us a life in slavery today, a slavery that feeds the "free world" (and often our pets) a steady supply of fish and fishmeal. The export of shrimp and fish from Southeast Asia has grown rapidly in the past decade and is now an industry worth many billions of dollars—a large part of the fish and shrimp we eat reaches us from the hands of people like Vannak. The billions we spend flow to multinational companies, large local businesses in Thailand and other countries, and into the pockets of slaveholders. The seafood here is cheap because laborers there are forced to work without pay.

Vannak, in spite of his years enduring brutality and suffering, is one of the lucky ones. He survived and was able to return to his family. He is slowly recovering from the trauma of slavery, and that recovery is helped along by his ability to express, explain, draw, and present to others his ordeal, his journey into and out of slavery. This startling blend of art and words is a profound gift to us. Understanding slavery is desperately hard if you have only known freedom.

It is easy to cast judgments on the basis of our own free will: "Why didn't he just run away?" or "Why didn't he fight back?" The answer is here; the truth of slavery is here in Vannak's words and art. In a world where slaves and survivors of slavery are regularly silenced, Vannak opens our eyes and ears to the nearly unimaginable.

KEVIN BALES
ST SAVIOUR, GUERNSEY, NOVEMBER 1, 2017

CONTRIBUTOR BIOS

ANNE ELIZABETH MOORE was born in Winner, South Dakota. She is the author of *Unmarketable*, *Cambodian Grrrl*, and *Threadbare*, and the former editor of *Punk Planet, The Comics Journal*, the *LA Review of Books* comics section, and the *Best American Comics* series from Houghton Mifflin. The Fulbright Senior Scholar and her cat Thurber—Chicagoans by disposition—were recently awarded the third Write A House fellowship in Detroit, Michigan. Her *Truthout* comics journalism series on that city with Melissa Mendes was recently granted a National Endowment for the Arts award.

MINKY WORDEN, Human Rights Watch's Director of Global Initiatives, develops and implements international outreach and advocacy campaigns, and works with journalists to help them cover crises, wars, human rights abuses, and political developments in some 90 countries worldwide. Worden has been Adjunct Associate Professor of International and Public Affairs at Columbia University since 2013. Before joining Human Rights Watch in 1998, Worden lived and worked in Hong Kong as an adviser to Democratic Party chairman Martin Lee and worked at the US Department of Justice. She is the editor of *The Unfinished Revolution and China's Great Leap*, and the co-editor of *Torture*. She serves on the board of the Human Trafficking Legal Center.

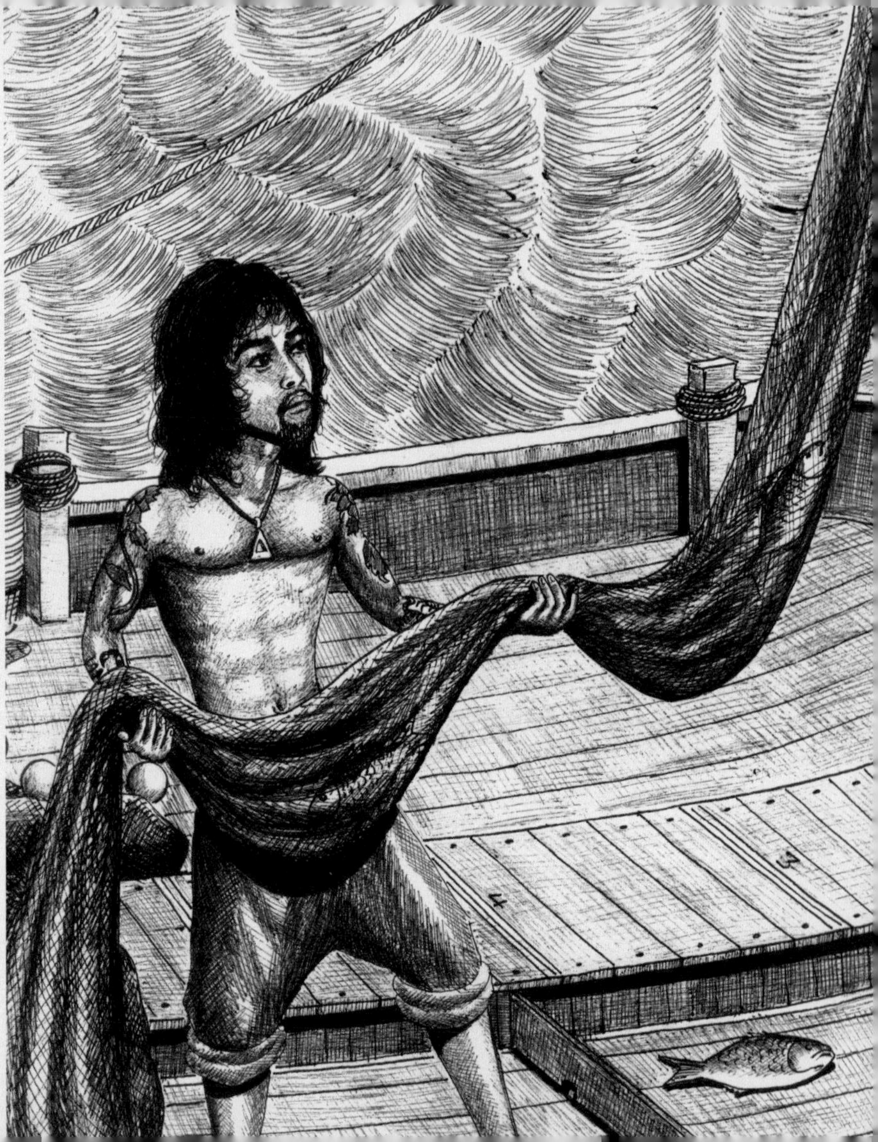

KEVIN BALES is Professor of Contemporary Slavery, and Research Director at the Rights Lab, at the University of Nottingham. In 2000 he cofounded Free the Slaves, a group that has helped liberate thousands of enslaved people worldwide. For his first book, *Disposable People*, Bales went undercover to meet slaves and slaveholders, investigating and exposing modern slavery's role in the global economy. His latest book, *Blood and Earth*, explores the deadly link between slavery and environmental destruction, with a special focus on the Southeast Asian fishing industry.

JOCELYN and **BEN PEDERICK** have been working side by side with Vannak Prum to tell his story since 2011, when Jocelyn first reported on Vannak's experience for Radio Free Asia. Jocelyn and Ben are co-founders of Goodmorningbeautiful Films, based in Cambodia, Sierra Leone, and Australia. GMBFilms are collaborating with Vannak to adapt his story into a film.

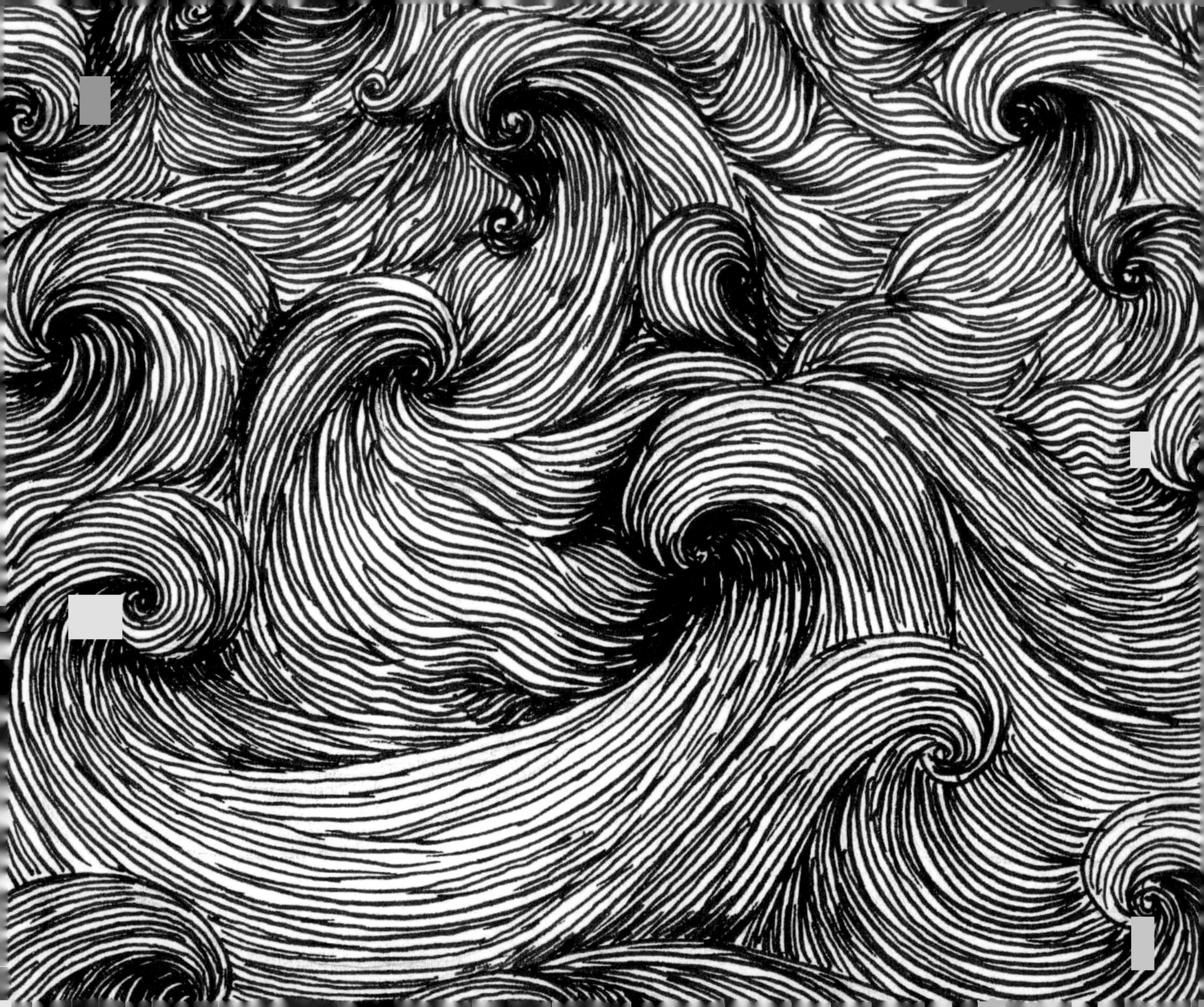